Stanwyck

Also by Jane Ellen Wayne

Stanwyck

Jane Ellen Wayne

Arbor House / *New York*

For Elizabeth and Mickey,
my dearest friends

Unless otherwise indicated, all photographs are from the
author's personal collection.

Manufactured in the United States of America

10   9   8   7   6   5   4   3   2   1

Designed by Richard Oriolo

Library of Congress Cataloging in Publication Data

Wayne, Jane Ellen.
Stanwyck.

Filmography: p. 201
1. Stanwyck, Barbara, 1907–   . 2. Moving-
pictures actors and actresses—United States—Biography.
I. Title.
PN2287.S67W3   1985   791.43′028′0924   [B]   85-18518
ISBN 0-87795-750-9

June 11, 1969

O n a warm Wednesday in Glendale, California, June 11, 1969, an organ chimed "Some Enchanted Evening," romantic, sentimental, touching. But people were not dancing or singing. They were paying their respects.

In Forest Lawn's tiny Church of the Recessional sat a select few friends. Among them were some well-known faces—Van Heflin, Dale Robertson, Walter Pidgeon, Robert Stack—all lost in reflection while they waited for the brief service to begin.

The beautiful German-born widow entered the family vestibule followed by her two children, both fair and blond in contrast to their parents.

As "I'll Get By" echoed through the Rudyard Kipling Gardens that hugged the stone chapel, a slender silver-haired woman made her slow, regal entrance, held up by two men. She wore a yellow suit because her husband had once told her, "Don't wear black to my funeral." She was late and her entrance spectacular. All eyes were on her, a rarity in Hollywood, where everyone had seen it all. These few minutes, however, were irritating to many, pathetic to some, and shocking to all.

Although she had been invited to join the family in private, she chose the main chapel, and the other mourners wondered why. If pride prevented her from doing so, it did nothing to conceal the red and swollen eyes. Those who observed Barbara Stanwyck that day said no one else showed the grief she openly displayed. Van Heflin thought she disrupted the service before it began. In her own deliberate way, she dominated the chapel by not sitting in the back or with the family out of sight. Robert Taylor was dead. During and after their divorce she repeated, "There will be no other man in my life."

And there never was.

Robert Taylor was dead.

The eulogy was given by another dear friend, Governor Ronald Reagan, who barely made it through without breaking down as he spoke the words: "I know some night on the late late show I'm going to see Bob resplendent in white tie and tails at Delmonico's, and I'm sure I'll smile—smile at Robert Spangler Arlington Brugh Taylor, because I'll remember how a fellow named Bob really preferred blue jeans and boots. And I'll see him squinting through the smoke of a barbecue as I have seen him a hundred times. He loved his home and everything that it meant. Above all, he loved his family and his beautiful Ursula—little Tessa; Terry, his son, a young man in whom he had so much pride."

At this point Barbara wept openly and unashamedly after having sobbed throughout the eulogy. The others could not help looking at her, and the loud tears affected Reagan's ability to continue as the Reverend Demarest moved restlessly in his chair.

Reagan choked with emotion, continued, "In a little while the hurt will be gone. Time will do that for you. Then you will find you can bring out your memories. You can look at them—take comfort from their warmth. As the years go by, you will be very proud."

Then Reagan turned to the family vestibule: "Bob spoke to me just a few days ago. I am sure he meant for me to tell you something that he wanted above all else. Ursula, there is just one last thing that only you can do for him—be happy. This was his last thought to me."

Each heart in the chapel stirred for the hidden Ursula, who had lost her son by a previous marriage less than a month before Bob died. But again it was Barbara Stanwyck who drew all the attention. After the eulogy was finished, no one moved until she stood up and almost in a faint was ushered out of the church. As flashbulbs popped in her face, she nearly passed out.

Tom Purvis, Taylor's navy buddy and close friend, was relieved when she finally got into the limousine safely. He had known Taylor for twenty-five years, but had seen Barbara only once or twice. "She didn't like me and I didn't like her for no particular reason than she resented all of his friends. They weren't welcome in the house when she was married to Bob. Why the hell she came to the funeral in such a pitiful state, I don't know. Bob would not have appreciated it.

"We were all invited to Taylor's house for a 'drink on him,' a Hollywood tradition. It's a final gathering for friends who had one friend in common and a nice gesture. Not being in show business, I didn't understand the whole concept, but Bob once told me it was a way of saying thanks and good-bye at home.

"I was damned shocked when Barbara walked in. First thing I said to myself was that Bob would not have allowed this. He never wanted her as a guest at his Ursulor Rancho. Then I was told it was Ursula who had extended the invitation.

"I thought it was odd that she would sit with Manuela Thiess, Bob's stepdaughter, who also was a misfit that day. Taylor was very proud of his ranch and his kids. He did not appreciate trespassers, but these two were. Neither one of them could share memories of Bob, so they were left alone. When Barbara left, I felt we could at last chat openly about the good times, and then I looked out the front window and saw Barbara with Ursula. There we were, a group of men peering out of windows without being seen to make sure Ursula was all right. She had been through hell and did not need Barbara to add to the tragedies. They walked round and round the circular driveway and Barbara was doing all the talking. About what, everyone asked. And why?"

This private conversation ended under a magnolia tree, all eyes waiting for a display of tears. But the two women just parted, no brief hug or handshake, no kiss on the cheek or fond farewell. To the relief of everyone, the first Mrs. Robert Taylor's limousine eased down the dusty driveway and away from the house.

No one ever found out what they spoke about. Ursula was not upset and indicated that Barbara was not at at all the way Bob described her. She could not understand why he went out of his way to avoid his first wife and absolutely refused to invite her to his home. But one year later Ursula Thiess Taylor would find out her late husband knew very well what he was doing.

It is ironic that the one man Barbara Stanwyck would love forever could not stand the sight of her. Frank Fay, her first husband, is dead, but he too showed little if any respect for her. Both men refused to talk about her. Taylor's only comment was, "You don't know Barbara the way I do," and he left it at that. When his agents committed him to the 1965 film *The Night Walker* costarring his ex-wife, he exploded, but could do nothing about the commitment. He told reporters, "Who could pass up the opportunity of working with such a wonderful talented woman?"

He could. The only truthful word in his statement was "talented," and no one who has ever worked with her will deny that—unless it was her other peers, who nominated her for an Oscar four times but never gave her one. Those who worked with her had only praise because she was a perfectionist and a dedicated actress. She memorized the entire script before beginning a film—and that included everyone's lines. Laurence Harvey said, "I never did know which side of the camera she was working."

In later years she won an Emmy and was given a special Oscar, among other awards, for her ability as an actress. No one deserved them more—or needed them more. They cost her the love of her adopted son and the husband she worshiped. Above all, her career came first.

She has been asked many times to write her memoirs and declined because she could not bear to talk about Robert Taylor. One writer almost got an interview, but only when he listed the questions he was going to ask and pledged not to deviate. She hesitated a long time before finally agreeing. The writer swore he only wanted to know about the Golden Era of Hollywood and nothing personal, but at the last minute she refused to see him "because Robert Taylor is part of that era."

Her story is remarkable, heart-stirring, shocking, and sad. Barbara Stanwyck had it all, but she clawed her way to the top, inch by inch. She was shunned and humiliated, but she never gave up.

She spent hours at the zoo watching the panthers, pacing with them, moving like them—silently, easily, royally. Assuredly. And her five-foot-five-inch frame stood taller than that of any rugged actor. Her diminutive 115 pounds outweighed her two husbands.

Robert Taylor said, "There were two traits I admired in Barbara and Garbo. Barbara turned off anyone who crossed her once. Garbo demanded her privacy and got it. I was too young at the time to understand how they stuck to their guns and never relented."

* * *

Ruby Stevens was an orphan from Brooklyn, New York, alone and frightened. Today she's known as Barbara Stanwyck from Beverly Hills, alone and frightened.

How far is it from foster homes in Brooklyn to Trousdale Estates in California?

"It is a long road with a lot of bumps and rocks in it."

One

 $\mathcal{B}$arbara Stanwyck was born Ruby Stevens on July 16, 1907, in Brooklyn, New York.

Her mother, Catherine McGee, had been brought up in Chelsea, Massachusetts, where her Irish immigrant parents settled. She married a fisherman, Byron Stevens, when she was about twenty years old. Daughters Maude and Mabel were born less than a year apart, followed by Mildred, then finally Malcolm Byron (Byron Jr.) in 1905. Catherine stayed home to care for the four children while her husband tried to make a living as a fisherman. When this was not possible, he found odd jobs in construction and became an expert bricklayer.

The red-haired and handsome Byron, however, was a restless man. Moody and a heavy drinker, he was known for his Jekyll and Hyde personality. Sometimes he was quiet and unassuming, but more often his bad temper flared, exploding into violence. Byron began to resent being a poor man tied down struggling to support a wife and four children. The sailors who came into the port of Chelsea described life in the big cities, where there was money to be made. The houses and stores were different and the living was better. There were good opportunities for work, too.

Without explanation or warning, Byron Stevens deserted his family one night.

Catherine had many reasons for wanting him back. She was a devout Catholic and believed in the sanctity of marriage. He was the father of her children and she loved him. And she had four children who needed food, clothes, and shelter. By talking to some of the men he had worked with, Catherine was able to find her husband.

Byron was working as a bricklayer in Brooklyn. There was nothing he could do when Catherine and the children showed up. Enjoying life as a single man, he resented having to settle down again, but Catherine made the family comfortable at 246 Classon Avenue in Brooklyn.

Maude and Mabel got married and moved out, which eased things in the overcrowded house and helped alleviate the financial strain on their father. But then Catherine discovered she was pregnant, and early in 1907 Byron found himself out of work and the pressure began building up again. On July 16 a daughter, Ruby, was born. Byron did odd jobs while Catherine concentrated on keeping her family fed and, above all, together.

The Stevens children lived in an environment of poverty. They considered the train whistles down the street something all children heard in the middle of the night. Although they were punished severely if they dared to cross the railroad tracks, they were allowed to walk around the waterfront and watch the ships come and go. It was cool there, and if they pretended hard enough, for a while they could forget the garbage and clotheslines at home. In this neighborhood women in their twenties looked thirty years older as they scrubbed floors with old rags, cooked in huge black pots, and carried their newborn babies under one arm while they hung up cloth diapers that never got clean.

Two years after Ruby was born, Catherine discovered she was pregnant with her sixth child. If Byron felt closed in before, he was smothered now. It wasn't the happiest of times. Byron's mind was thousands of miles away; drinking and dreaming, he refused to accept that this was his life forever.

In 1910 his world fell apart when Catherine, soon to give birth, stepped off a trolley car and was accidentally pushed in the street. She hit her head and was unconscious until she died a week later. Byron could not face taking care of three children and working at hard labor just to make ends meet. It was hopeless. A few weeks after Catherine's funeral, he disappeared again, but no one followed him this time. The last anyone heard was that he was working on the Panama Canal as a bricklayer.

Mildred, who had been working as a chorus girl, knew her father would not send money to support Ruby and Byron Jr. She was sure they would never see him again, but whether they did or not, something had to be done immediately. She got no help from Maude and Mabel, who claimed to have their own problems.

So Ruby and Byron Jr. were placed in foster homes, which might not have been so awful had the two been able to be together. Looking on the bright side, the distance between the two houses was only a few blocks. At five, Byron found it difficult to take, but he was more concerned about his three-year-old sister—who ran away every afternoon.

He knew where to find Ruby: she would be playing on the sidewalk in front of 246 Classon Avenue, looking for her mother. The young children did not suffer abuse from their foster parents, but as Stanwyck herself described it, "It wasn't quite as bad as it sounded. In those days foster homes were not cruel. They were just impersonal."

Ruby and Byron went from foster home to foster home, sometimes together, sometimes not, but always close enough to be with each other every day. They said later in life that if it had not been for the other, they could not have come out of it as well as they did. The elder sisters visited whenever they could, which wasn't often. Mildred was traveling as a dancer, but continued to support her brother and sister and look after them whenever she was in New York, enjoying her visits with them.

But one visit she would have liked to avoid was the time she came to tell Ruby and Byron their father had died at sea. They preferred to believe he was coming home to see them. Stanwyck said she wasn't quite sure when they became orphans "officially," but it was when she was about five.

Stanwyck later said she could accept being shuffled from one strange home to another and even the death of a father she never knew, but when she was eight years old, her whole world fell apart. "My sister Mildred thought Byron was old enough to live with her. I did everything I could. I cried and I wanted to run away with him. Then I begged Mildred to take me, too. I pleaded and I screamed, but she took him anyway."

Ruby would have to confront the world alone now, and that's exactly what she did. Without Byron to protect her, she fought her own battles on the street, adopted foul language, and in general became rebellious and contentious. She had no close friendships because she trusted no one. She never developed affection for any of her foster parents. She slept on a cot, usually in the living room, ate her meals, went to school, played on the street, and went to bed. Without much notice she was moved to another foster home and enrolled into another school. "I was a stupid brat," she said, "but cared less."

Girls did not care for Ruby Stevens and she, in turn, did not care for them. She was a scrapper and a wiz at the street games that boys played. They liked her because of her spunk, and this was one reason she got along with men better than women throughout her life.

If Ruby had anything to look forward to, it was going on the road with Mildred during the summer. The tough, young, lonely Ruby was thrilled by the dancers and wanted to be one herself. She picked up whatever steps she could and practiced them at home. School meant nothing to her—as far as she was concerned, she had no real use for reading, writing, and arithmetic.

Soon summer was over and Mildred had to go on the road again for the winter months. She found a nicer home for Ruby this time and encouraged her to love the Cohen family, who would look upon her as something more than a foster child. Ruby, of course, believed no one, not even Mildred. As far as she was concerned, the Cohens were just another couple making a buck on taking in an orphan.

But if Ruby ever felt like an adored and welcome little girl, it was in the Cohen household. "Not only was the house clean, but it was full of sincere love and they were always concerned about me. I wasn't sent to school without my hair being combed and my face scrubbed and without clean clothes. The Cohens were rather poor, but they fed me well and took me to church and sometimes to the movies."

Maybe the Cohens were able to make Ruby look like a little lady, but they could not make her talk like one. Every other sentence contained a curse word, and though reprimanded every time she swore, using dirty words was as much of her personality as everything else she had picked up on the streets. The Cohens did not give up, and they did succeed in changing Ruby.

After two years of a normal life for Ruby, Mrs. Cohen became pregnant. Ruby did not have to be told there would be no room for her. She made up her mind to quit school and get a job.

Ruby lied about her age and got a job at the Condé Nast outfit. She also lied about being able to cut out patterns. When she failed and got fired, she went through the want ads in the newspapers and applied for a job as a typist at the Remick Music Publishing Company on Forty-eighth Street in Manhattan. She minded her own business and made few friends except for Bill Cripp, the manager, who had hired her. It's not clear whether she trusted him because he trusted her or because she merely needed someone to confide in, but she told him her ambition was to be a dancer. This time her faith in someone paid off: Cripp got her an audition at the Strand Theater in Times Square as a dancer, paying thirty-five dollars a week. The dance director, Earl Lindsay, hired her and gave her her first professional training as a dancer.

She knew she had talent, and she was aware that the competition was keen. But she was determined to be a somebody. For the time being she would rely on dedication and eagerness to learn. She became the most reliable girl in the chorus line. Because she came from the streets, she was able to handle most of the mashers—quipping with them, putting them down, or at least holding them off. But she was abused from time to time. More than once her costume was ripped down the front by mashers waiting in the wings.

Ruby was a thin girl with few curves, and her legs left a lot to be desired. But she had the spunk and the will, and if she moved and kicked fast enough, her figure wasn't important. And she *was* attractive, with her pretty auburn hair and blue eyes.

Never one to chat with the girls about anything personal, she nevertheless listened and tried to learn the ropes. Though she had not known her father, Ruby took after him—rough, ambitious, restless, loud, sarcastic, frank, and uncaring. She would grow to be more like the Stevens side.

As she gained confidence as a dancer at the Strand, she became friendlier with the other girls, becoming especially close to Mae Clark and Walda Mansfield, who eventually became her roommates in a cold-water flat on Forty-sixth Street between Fifth and Sixth avenues.

"This was my first real home," she remembers. "We lived over a laundry, which could be steamy at times and especially hot during the summer. The heat seemed to come through every crack in the floor and ceiling. Then there was the noisy Sixty Avenue El that shook the walls. Sometimes we felt like we could reach out and touch the trains. Of course, we were in a glamorous business, so we couldn't allow our dates to see the joint so we told them to drop us off at one of the hotels in the theater district and pretend we lived there. Even in the early twenties forty dollars a week only covered necessities and sometimes not even that."

When the show at the Strand closed, the girls went to work for Earl Lindsay in *Keep Kool* at the Morosco Theater. The official opening was May 22, 1924. Ruby was one of the Keep Kool Cuties. *Variety* gave them a good review: "These sixteen girls are pips, lookers and dancers. They kick like steers and look like why-men-leave-home in their many costume flashes."

Keep Kool featured the famous Hazel Dawn, and Ruby was given a specialty number with Johnny Dooley called "A Room Adjoining a Boudoir." When the show closed in August, Ziegfeld decided to take some of the sketches on his *Follies* road show. He gave Ruby $100 a week, and part of her dream had come true. The orphan from the streets of Brooklyn was an official Ziegfeld Girl! In the famous "Ziegfeld Shadowgraph" number she did a strip-tease behind a white screen. "I tossed my clothes out into the audience. But if they did not wear three-dimensional glasses, they didn't get to see anything." The roaring twenties were in high gear and Ruby Stevens was in the middle of it: speakeasies, bootleg booze, sensual dances, short skirts, low necklines, fast music, and fast girls.

When the Ziegfeld *Follies* tour ended, Ruby had no

problem finding a job. She accepted an offer by the Anatole Friedland's Club on Fifty-fourth Street. Six months
later she and Mae Clark were let go when business declined. But Earl Lindsay came to the rescue with *Gay
Paree* starring Ruth Gillette and Billy Van. Now Ruby
added a Shubert revue to her list of credits. At the same
time she and Mae were offered a job dancing at a little
after-hours dump called the Everglades Café. They ran
from one job to the other, sometimes wearing only coat
and shoes in the bitter cold of January 1926. But their luck
didn't last, and several months later they were both out of
work.

She and Mae hung out at the Tavern on Forty-eighth
Street and mingled with other show business people. The
owner, Billy LaHiff, who was sympathetic toward young
hopefuls out of work, allowed them to run up a tab or fed
them for nothing. Billy was indirectly responsible for the
remarkable transformation of Ruby Stevens into the leg-
endary Barbara Stanwyck.

Billy was the one who introduced Ruby to Willard
Mack, a producer, director, playwright, and star. Mack,
who at the time was casting for *The Noose,* hired her on
the spot as a chorus girl. As the legend goes, Ruby stuck
her neck out and said she would accept only if he hired
her two roommates as well. He agreed.

They opened in Pittsburgh and the play was a turkey,
so Mack revised the script and shuffled the cast into different roles. He gave Ruby a juicy acting part in the third
act. She was elated but also frightened, because she was
only a hoofer. The few lines she spoke in the original play
were barely worth thinking about, but now Mack was
asking her to carry the entire third act.

Mack was no fool. He saw something in Ruby. She had
guts and spirit, a good foundation for trying to save the
play and make it a success on Broadway.

Stanwyck recalled these hectic weeks: "Willard Mack

showed me all the tricks, how to sell myself with entrances and exits. Only through his kindness and patience
did I make it through. He completely disarranged my
mental makeup. It was a rebirth. I guess pretty damn
painful, especially for him. I was temperamental, but I
was scared. I told him I couldn't act—that it was hopeless.
I couldn't and what's more, I wouldn't! Then Mr. Mack
did a turnabout, and in front of the entire company he
said I was a chorus girl and would always be a chorus girl,
would live like a chorus girl, so to hell with me! It worked.
I yelled back that I could act, would act, and was not just a
chorus girl!"

But before she signed her contract, Mack did her another favor, saying, "Ruby Stevens is no name for an actress." Then he began looking through an old English
theater program, which listed Jane Stanwyck in *Barbara
Frietchi*. Almost immediately he hit upon it: "From now
on you'll be known as Barbara Stanwyck."

As she was about to sign her name, she got as far as
"Bar," looked up at Mack, and asked, "How do you spell
Barbara?" From that moment on she always used two
capital B's in her first name—BarBara.

The Noose was a story about a young man condemned
to death, a society girl, and a chorus girl/dancer. In the
original script the society girl pleads for the body of the
man she loves. Mack's drastic change in the script called
for the chorus girl—Stanwyck—to plead with the governor for the young man's body. The young man loved
someone else, she tells the governor, but she would bury
him and over his grave tell him the many things she dared
not say while he was alive. When she finds out the
doomed young man is still alive, that his execution has
been stayed, she begs the governor not to say anything
about her visit.

Mack had attempted to hire an experienced stage actress for the part when the script was revised, but the

women he chose had other commitments and he was forced to use Ruby. He never doubted her ability, but her facing a New York audience for the first time was a nerve-wracking event for him. Countless rehearsals and careful preparations did not guarantee a worthy performance—especially by a newcomer.

Mack was more than just fond of Ruby. Their close relationship lasted for many years, and she had deep affection for him. His attraction to Ruby sorted her out from the others who might easily have been chosen for the bit role in the first version. She was, after all, a dancer with no ambition to become an actress. Ruby had little regard for herself as an intellect or well-spoken young woman, and she never lost her Brooklyn accent. Nor was she aware of social graces or good manners. When she wasn't dancing, she moved awkwardly with a heavy stride, arms swinging back and forth like a Russian soldier.

Her only qualification for the role was the few speaking parts she had in slapstick. Mack was too professional for last-minute decisions. By offering her the role, he had her in his clutches. Ruby had no idea what was happening to her.

But she was going to go through with a juicy piece of acting in a leading play—and do it with determination and guts. What did she have to lose? If she bombed as an actress, she was still a good hoofer.

She surprised everyone when *The Noose* opened on October 20, 1926, at the Hudson Theater on Broadway. It was a smash—and the beginning of an amazing career.

The *New York Telegram* said: "There is an uncommonly fine performance by Barbara Stanwyck, who not only does the Charleston steps of a dance hall girl gracefully, but knows how to act, a feature which somehow with her comely looks seems kind of superfluous. After this girl breaks down and sobs out her unrequited love for the young bootlegger in that genuinely moving scene in the last act, of course, there is nothing for the Governor to do but reprieve the boy. If he hadn't, the weeping audience would probably have yelled at him till he did."

Billboard raved: "Barbara Stanwyck is splendid as the leader of the little chorus and she achieves real heights in her brief emotional scene." The *New York Sun* reported that she made first-nighters wipe tears from their eyes. The *New York Times* referred to her as Dorothy Stanwyck, but said she did "good work."

One story that circulated was about Ruby's sister Mildred, who was invited to the play's opening night. Unaware that Barbara Stanwyck was actually her sister, Mildred sat patiently through the show but left before the last act. Regardless of the truth, it was amusing publicity.

If Mack was proud of Barbara, he made sure not to offer too much praise. Did she want to become a good actress? Or did she prefer dancing? Her answer was, "Acting!" Mack wasn't surprised. "Then we have a lot to do," he said. Although *The Noose* ran on Broadway for nine months, he gave her a different play to study every week and they rehearsed together. Mack also insisted she rehearse her lines in *The Noose* every morning at the theater.

The untamed orphan from Brooklyn, it would seem, had little time for a social life. Barbara wasn't running with flashy admirers anymore because she had fallen in love with her leading man, Rex Cherryman. "I had been dating a young chap by the name of Edward Kennedy and we almost got married, but when I became seriously interested in acting, I felt we should wait. Then I met Rex Cherryman, who changed all that. Edward always suspected I was in love with Willard Mack, and although there was a deep professional commitment there, it was Rex I loved. He was very handsome, had enormous talent and a wonderful sense of humor." Women chased him, and he took advantage of it until he became intrigued with

Barbara, who was different from the rest. She was unpretentious, brassy, unaware of her attractiveness, and innocent in the ways of love. Although she worshiped him in the beginning, she had no idea he would pay any attention to her, and when he did, she was awkward and silly. Apparently Rex found this refreshing and different. They became a steady couple and as Barbara described it later: "It was simple. He was the first man I adored and it was all so perfect. We were both becoming established Broadway performers and understood each other very well."

While still performing in *The Noose*, Barbara was asked to make a screen test at the old Cosmopolitan Studios on 125th Street and Second Avenue for the silent movie *Broadway Nights*. She said it was a horrible experience because the cameraman tried to make a date with her while she was trying to get into the right mood for the test. The director didn't care that she was being pawed because his only concern was that she be able to cry in her role. He handed her a raw onion just as the famous actress Ruth Chatterton walked in. The camera rolled, but Barbara could not get the tears to flow—the sad violin wailing in the background and the smell of onion in her nostrils did nothing to help her cry. When Chatterton remarked that a screen test must surely be a flop "when a movie actress has to resort to onions and violins," Stanwyck told her to shut up and attempted to finish. Someone else on the set told Chatterton: "That dumb actress you're referring to is giving a magnificent performance by crying each night in *The Noose* and does it so effectively that there is not one dry eye in the audience!"

Stanwyck did not get the part she tried out for, but did get a minor role and fifth billing. She does not list this film as one of her credits. Sylvia Sidney also made her screen debut in *Broadway Nights*.

Looking back, Stanwyck said it was not her performance in the original test that was so terrible. She was good considering the fact it took her awhile to shed tears, but the obnoxious cameraman photographed her badly. It was, according to a witness, a mess, but even as a green kid Stanwyck could overcome heckling, pressure, and her own inability to perform on cue.

The Noose closed in June 1927, and a few weeks later Stanwyck auditioned for a part in George Manker Watter's Broadway play, *Burlesque* with vaudevillian Hal Skelly. The producer of this play said she was perfect for the part. "Stanwyck had a rough poignancy and she displayed sensitivity and emotion far superior than some of the great actresses I've known."

Her role as a drunken vaudevillian's wife who returns to save him in the end was another demanding part. *Burlesque* opened on September 1, 1927, at the Plymouth Theater and was a smash.

"I owed my performance in my second play to Arthur Hopkins, the director, who took me by the hand just the way Mack did," she said. "I had a feeling that everything he told me to do was right. He never really told me what to do. Instead he told me stories and let me imagine how it should be and how I would feel in these particular situations. Then I went about it in my own way and it always worked."

This was Stanwyck's natural ability, the natural ability that would eventually make her a legend. Mack taught her the basics and gave her the formulas, but it was Hopkins who let her go about it naturally. Other directors would discover similar qualities in Stanwyck, but she owes most of her success to these two directors.

Alexander Woollcott reviewed *Burlesque* in *The World*. "Miss Stanwyck's performance was touching and true and she brought much to those little aching silences in a performance of which Mr. Hopkins knows so well, the secret and the sorcery."

Her second and most successful play underway, Barbara was very much in the public eye and reporters wanted to know more about her role in *Burlesque*. She was quoted in an interview for *New York Review:* "How can you explain love anyway? You can't. It is one of those things you recognize and you know it exists, but seek the reason and you are up a tree. They say pity is akin to love and I suppose that has a great deal to do with Bonny's feeling for her husband in the play. He needed someone badly to look after him and I guess Bonny knew she had been elected for the job of loving this poor clown. I have often thought of what the finish would be for these two people—what old age would bring to them. People are the most interesting things in life. Ordinarily we do not appreciate this fact, but when we walk away from a play like this, we have the feeling that we have been unobserving of the world around us, and life holds a great deal more for us all than we thought."

It is unlikely that Stanwyck thought up this profound approach to life on her own in 1927. She was coached by Hopkins, who gave her the ideas and told her how to put them into words. She was far from distinguished and polished off the stage. She continued to express herself like a hoofer and it would take time to make over Ruby Stevens into Barbara Stanwyck. At the age of twenty with little education or experience, she was more capable in character than out, which is true of many actors and actresses. Off stage she was not sure of herself and was more confident repeating lines given to her. Later in life, when she was one of the most popular actresses in the world, she admitted that expressing herself was difficult and often impossible. Her interviews left a great deal to be desired, though she always came to the point. Tact was not one of her virtues.

Although life was treating her well in 1928, she remembered a lesson she had learned when she was a foster child living with the Cohen family. Too good to last very

long. Her career flourishing and her relationship with Rex
Cherryman becoming serious, she could not ask for more.
Rex became ill, however, and his performance in *The
Trial of Mary Dugan* was cut short so that he could take a
recuperative vacation in Europe. Barbara wept at the dock
as his ship pulled out, and looked forward to meeting him
abroad when *Burlesque* closed.

On the way to Europe Rex had a relapse and died in a
Le Havre hospital at the age of thirty, a severe setback for
Barbara. For a long time she wondered why the people
closest to her died at such an early age. It was not easy for
her to love and trust. Rex Cherryman did not let her
down any more than Mrs. Cohen had when she became
pregnant. It was, Barbara concluded, just her bad luck and
a lousy turn of fate. Alone, again.

Her only salvation was to dig deeper into her career, to
maintain her determination and learning and practice,
which had paid off so far. If you want it done, do it yourself, that was her motto. She would beg and plead and
crawl. No one could prevent her from doing that. Nor
could anyone take away the credits she had already
earned. If love was not in her grasp, she could do without
it. When you're accustomed to not knowing if you were
going to have a bed that night or supper on the table, love
and marriage were secondary. She could rely on herself
from now on because no one had given her anything she
hadn't deserved. She would have to be tough, though, and
make sure those who would stand in her way knew just
how tough she was.

The death of Rex Cherryman made her tougher than
ever. She doubted that she would be able to give herself to
any man as she had to Rex. Whatever effort and strength
she had put into this doomed affair, she would add to her
spirit and guts to fulfill the dream that now was so close
she could almost grasp it—success as an actress. Nothing
would stand in her way. And nothing ever did.

TWO

Stanwyck and Cherryman were a popular couple in the little clubs on New York's West Side, and it had been assumed by the show business crowd that they would get married. His death was a shock to everyone in the theater and, though they expressed their sympathy, Barbara was devastated. Work was her only salvation, but going through her paces like a robot, she had to face those hours alone. As the weeks passed, her determination and strength waned as she realized how desperately she needed Rex. When she was with him, she felt warm and safe. Had she ever been cuddled and held as a child? Or knew the security of an adoring eye from across the room?

Never until Rex Cherryman.

Unable to pull herself together when she was not performing, other members of the cast began to worry about her, the fighter who was losing this round.

There was one person, however, who was able to give her the comfort and closeness she craved: "Broadway's Favorite Son," Frank Fay. They disliked each other from the beginning, so it is ironic that he should be the one who saved her from herself. Oscar Levant, the piano player in *Burlesque*, arranged for her to watch Fay from the wings of the Palace Theater and introduced them after the show.

Barbara was far from awed by Fay's enormous ego. She told Levant, "I saw him perform a year ago. It's real apparent he loves himself. He's his own biggest fan and never shuts up." Levant said Fay was the hottest thing on Broadway and breaking all records at the Palace. "Yeah?" she smirked. "That doesn't mean I have to like him."

Levant passed this on to Fay, who sarcastically countered that Stanwyck was nothing to get excited about either.

Fay in many ways resembled Barbara's father, Byron Stevens. He had red hair and never stood still. Divorced twice, he was a ladies' man who bragged about his conquests. Like Byron, Fay had a fierce Irish temper, a sharp tongue, and he was always hyper and thoroughly self-centered.

To compound the family resemblance, Fay was as brassy and insulting as she was. Knowing what each thought of the other, they kept up a sarcastic flow of bantering barbs and counterbarbs whenever they ran into each other. They both knew the language of the street and it was no-holds-barred, each vying for the last insult.

"I can't stand him," she told anyone within hearing range.

Fay, on the other hand, rarely met anyone, especially a woman, who could keep up with him. He could swear like a sailor and she could do better. He was loud and she could be louder. He was always on stage and she never missed a beat. He was Broadway's Favorite Son, and he spent every minute living up to that title. Barbara obviously saw through his bluster, though she said in later years she was in awe of Fay.

He had met his match and started to look forward to each verbal tug-of-war when they ran into each other on

Broadway. But Barbara was in love with Cherryman and busy with her career. Frank Fay, meanwhile, had no problem finding a different chorus girl every night.

The fact that both he and Barbara went out of their way to heckle each other indicated to observers that they enjoyed it more than either realized. He found himself attracted to her bluntness and was fascinated with her earthy personality. But it was not until Cherryman's death that Frank Fay came to Barbara as a friend and someone willing to help. They could communicate on the same level and she understood him. She also saw another side to Frank Fay—a guy who was willing to be with her when she needed him, listen to her talk endlessly about the great Rex Cherryman, and accept her for what she was.

Brokenhearted, she leaned on the sympathetic Fay, who had known for some time he was in love with Barbara, but was sensitive enough not to bring it up while she was still grieving. His enormous success represented confidence. Frank Fay knew where he was and where he was going. His bad habits were her bad habits. She could be Ruby Stevens with him, throw off her shoes, drink too much, and let herself go.

Francis Anthony Fay, suave archetype of the old Palace guard, was born to a vaudeville couple in San Francisco on November 17, 1896. He spent his life from the age of four in show business. He was a master of the studied insult, the raised eyebrow that could turn into a ribald double entendre, the droll aside that stung like a whiplash. His parody of the song "Tea for Two" (Who wants to bake a cake at three in the morning?) was a classic.

Fay made his debut on the stage as a potato bug, elf, or teddy bear—nobody could remember which—in Victor Herbert's *Babes in Toyland*. From there he played in *The Merchant of Venice* and *Louis IX*.

Early in his career Faysie, as his close friends called him, married singer Lee Buchanan. This marriage was short-lived. His second wife was the then reigning torch singer Frances White. They were divorced several years later.

In 1921, after a few years of diminished popularity, Fay hit bottom and filed a voluntary petition in bankruptcy, his only assets his $100 worth of clothes.

By developing the role of master of ceremonies into an art of wit, Fay made a comeback and in 1926 played the Palace for a hundred continuous performances, breaking all records. His stooge was Patsy Kelly, who went on to Hollywood fame.

Their classic vaudeville patter went like this:

"Where have you been?" Fay asked.

"At the beauty parlor."

"I see, and they didn't wait on you?"

Fay was a complex, fascinating, compelling fellow off-stage. Few knew he was a very religious man who attended mass every day, wore a Saint Christopher's medal around his neck, and always tipped his hat when he passed a house of worship. But he also read his horoscope every day; his friends used to ask him if he had more faith in God or in astrology. "I'm just covering all the bases," he would reply.

He drank and gambled freely. There was no happy medium for Frank Fay. Either he was rich or dead broke, sober or drunk, successful or bankrupt. Anything in between was dull to him.

He collected everything from antiques to unwashed socks worn by baseball heroes. Onstage he wore flamboyant dressing gowns, but in private he enjoyed leaning back in an easy chair wearing only a pair of shorts.

He was the kind of guy Ruby Stevens might have met on the streets in Brooklyn: Irish Catholic, rough and tumble, big-mouthed and cocksure.

* * *

Less than ten weeks after Rex Cherryman's death, Barbara Stanwyck boarded a train for Saint Louis, where Fay was appearing at the Missouri Theater. And on August 25, 1928, at one in the afternoon Barbara was married to Frank by the justice of the peace, witnessed by Spyros Skouros and Mrs. Harry Niemeyer. Four hours later the bride boarded another train for Newark, New Jersey, where *Burlesque* was beginning its national tour.

Fay had proposed to Barbara over the telephone. She would not suffer loneliness again. When Frank had left for the theater commitment in Saint Louis, she became distraught and desperately afraid she would lose the security she had found so soon after Cherryman's death. Barbara was reaching out and Frank extended his hand in marriage, offering her the salvation and love she had been seeking all her life. If she did not love him on their wedding day, it did not take her long to fall head over heels for Fay, an attractive man willing to be her lover, husband, and father. She gave herself completely to the man who could be all three.

If the couple had a strike against them, it was Fay's monumental ego. He did not relish competition—especially in his marriage. If his wife was going to remain in show business, it would be on his terms, and she was not to accept any jobs without his knowledge and approval. A conflict arose almost immediately when there was talk that Stanwyck would play the lead in the silent film version of *Burlesque* to be filmed at Paramount in Hollywood. Fay told her not to give out any information until he could follow through with some offers for himself. If they went to California, it was because the great Frank Fay was asked, not his wife.

Meanwhile she continued playing Bonny in the national tour of *Burlesque* until the show closed. She refused to discuss movie offers until Frank finally signed a contract with Warner Brothers to host several musicals entitled *Show of Shows.*

When word reached Hollywood that Fay and his wife were moving to California, Joseph Schenck, head of United Artists, came to New York and spoke with Barbara about doing the movie *The Locked Door* with Rod La Rocque and William Boyd. She happily agreed and he offered to take her and Frank to the West Coast in his private railroad car. Barbara tried to stay in the background and continue to give her husband "top billing" with whomever they met.

When they arrived in Hollywood, Douglas Fairbanks, Mary Pickford, and Norma Talmadge were waiting to greet Joe Schenck. This was quite a thrill for Barbara, but Fay was not impressed. He was going to take Hollywood by storm and make everyone else who thought they owned the place look two-bit compared to Broadway's Favorite Son!

Barbara did *The Locked Door,* a sound production of Channing Pollock's play *The Sign on the Door.* But she had arrived in Hollywood during the difficult transition from silent films to talkies. George Fitzmaurice, the director, was too concerned with technical problems to work with the performers. Barbara was on her own and unfamiliar with the art of moviemaking. She had been trained to project her voice and to exaggerate her body movements for the stage. No one bothered to tell her how to tone down for the microphone and camera.

In *The Locked Door* she portrayed the type of woman she would play many times in her career—the wicked girl with a past. Married to her boss (William Boyd), she is faced with her dark past when a former boyfriend shows up to ruin her life. The husband shoots her nasty ex-lover, but she is blamed. Fortunately the bad guy lives and tells the truth.

The *New York Herald Tribune* reported that "Barbara

Stanwyck gives an honest and moving picture as the distraught wife. . . . It is in every way an excellent piece of work."

Unfortunately this was the only positive revue or comment about *The Locked Door*. It was panned in general. Stanwyck said, "They never should've unlocked the damned thing!"

Disappointed with her Hollywood debut, she did a screen test for Warner Brothers but heard nothing. While she suffered seeing her name on the marquee in a film that was so dreadful, Stanwyck fumed.

"Nobody trained me for movies," she complained. "In the theater I had to reach the guys in the balcony and my arms and legs were stretched to accommodate the size of the stage. But on a small movie set, my voice was shrill and my walk was awkward. I was lost. Who the hell was going to teach me the ropes in this dizzy town?"

Her next film, *Mexicali Rose*, for Columbia was worse, if this was possible. Again she played an evil woman, but this time she is murdered for her unfaithfulness. Brooklyn accent and all, she played a Mexican girl—which just about sums up the results.

For a twenty-three-year-old girl who had started with nothing, yet managed to become a fine stage actress in two good plays, Stanwyck felt she had made a terrible mistake by coming to Hollywood. These two films were ruining her chances of acting again, in movies or on the stage. Without the proper training she made screen tests at the major studios and was completely ignored. A feeling of helplessness overcame her spunky enthusiasm and confidence.

For six months Barbara Stanwyck was virtually ignored. She never forgot those days when Hollywood snubbed her. Fame would not change her mind about the brutality in the movie industry.

An incident she would never forget occurred around

yet another screen test, this time the pleading-with-the-governor scene from *The Noose*. The director of the test was sad-faced, and not supported with a makeup man. After she did her famous scene, there were tears in his eyes, and he told her that although he was a failure and was leaving Hollywood, it was a privilege to experience such brilliant acting. The man—Alexander Korda, later to be knighted for such brilliant cinematic triumphs as *Rembrandt* and *The Private Lives of Henry VIII.*

The test was viewed and forgotten. Evidently, neither Mr. Korda nor Miss Stanwyck had anything to offer the movie industry.

During those long six months, she was just the wife of Frank Fay, big star busy making *Show of Shows* for Warner Brothers. The film was a success and Fay took most of the credit, even though he was only one reason for its success. As master of ceremonies he was bright-eyed, masterful, quick—and funny. Fay would never perform without complimenting himself in front of a live audience or before the camera. This was part of his act. Two more films, *The Matrimonial Bed* and *Under a Texas Moon* were pretty good, which meant excellent in Fay's mind. Concerning his wife, he was delighted to have her at home when he returned after a busy day at the studio. If she was depressed, it would pass. He would be successful enough for both of them, which is what he wanted—to be the star in the family and for his wife to take care of the house and remain in his shadow. At first Barbara convinced herself she could be happy being Mrs. Frank Fay and help boost him on the homefront. They enjoyed going out for dinner and to every party they were asked to attend; it was all part of the game. Anyway, Barbara did not know how to cook.

As the months passed, Fay was forced to face facts. His wife was depressed and her moods affected their marriage. She had no energy or desire for anything, and seeing her husband so enthusiastic only increased her sullen behavior. Very much in love with her, Fay wanted to help. He realized she was not happy sitting around doing nothing and, if she did bit parts every so often, what was the big deal?

He approached the head of Columbia Studios, the sarcastic and ruthless Harry Cohn. Fay offered to pay her salary and expenses personally if they would give her a chance. Cohn said the only film they might be able to use her in was *Ladies of Leisure*, but the director, Frank Capra, wanted nothing to do with Stanwyck. Cohn, who did not mince words, insisted on a routine interview and Capra agreed to the courtesy.

Frank couldn't wait to get home to tell Barbara, but she didn't bother to move from her chair or even say she was interested. As a matter of fact, she wasn't! One more rejection would defeat her completely. Fay urged her to keep the appointment.

Without changing out of her house dress, combing her hair, or putting on makeup, Stanwyck walked into Capra's office and plopped into a chair with a dejected and bored look on her face. She was the living embodiment of her two performances in *The Locked Door* and *Mexicali Rose*—drab and stupid.

He asked about her background and she responded unenthusiastically. The rest of the brief discussion was mumbling on her part. The bored Capra said the usual, "You'll have to make a screen test."

Suddenly her temper flared and she leaped out of the chair. "Oh hell, you don't want any part of me!" and slammed the door behind her.

Capra grabbed the phone and called Harry Cohn. "About that Stanwyck girl," he groaned. "She's not an actress. She's a porcupine!"

Barbara arrived home in tears—six months of frustration finally coming to the surface. If she felt better for

telling Capra off, it didn't show. She could not stop sobbing despite Fay's repeated questions about the interview.
Barbara continued weeping and was unable to talk. Fay's
mind drifted to the obvious director's "casting couch" and
all kinds of thoughts went through his head. Obviously
Barbara had been abused. Capra made a pass at her. In a
rage Fay picked up the phone and called Harry Cohn.

"What the hell did Capra do to my wife!" he yelled.

Cohn, known for his hot temper, shot back: "That
dame's got some kind of chip on her shoulder! Capra's a
gentleman and he tried to talk to her. Not only did she
look like hell, she acted like a child. Capra called her a
porcupine and do you know why, Fay? She stormed out
of Capra's office and slammed the door! Forget the whole
thing."

Fay calmed down because the description fit Barbara
perfectly. He explained to Cohn that his wife was just a
sensitive kid who had made a success on Broadway and
was pretty damned good. He dragged her to Hollywood
where she got kicked around and insulted. "She doesn't
have faith in anyone and I'm beginning to believe she
doesn't have any faith in me! I got one more favor and you
can't turn me down. I'm gonna show you a test Barbara
did at Warners. Don't go way!"

Cohn called in Capra, who definitely wasn't interested,
but before he could leave Cohn's office, Fay was there
with the film. Capra said that Stanwyck had so many
strikes against her he had already made up his mind to
hate the three-minute test. The fact that Fay got him to
watch it was in itself a miracle.

But he too had tears in his eyes. Rarely had he been so
impressed. He told Fay to sit tight and immediately got
Harry Cohn to sign Stanwyck for *Ladies of Leisure.*

Finally Barbara Stanwyck got the break so long in
coming. The role of a party girl who falls in love with a
society artist was made for her. The cheap wisecracks and

heavy makeup in the beginning and then the gradual transition to a gracious lady who desperately wants to be worthy of the man she loves is vintage Stanwyck.

Frank Capra, the director who initially could not tolerate her, made Barbara Stanwyck the great actress she was capable of becoming. It was during the filming of *Ladies of Leisure* that he made a remarkable discovery: he had, to his delight, a virgin actress. Her face was void of makeup, her hair untouched by hairdressers, and her personality just as plain and crude as it had been in Brooklyn. She wasn't interested in being beautiful or in which side of her face was in front of the camera or what she wore or how it looked on her. She was completely untouched. He could train her the right way because she was eager. The girl he met in his office the first time was not the girl who reported for work. The other Barbara—the real Barbara—was full of life and energy, anxious and willing, determined and alert.

Capra told Fay that his wife was a natural. Her talent lay in just being herself, and he wanted to keep her that way.

After shooting several scenes, Capra studied her on film. She had, of course, been made up for the camera and gave a stunning performance. Capra said she was gorgeous, but something was wrong. It was not the effect he was looking for. The following day, when she reported for work, the first thing Capra did was wash her face, and instruct her to be totally natural and not worry about her lines or her movement.

Capra liked what he saw and repeated each scene several times. He soon discovered another of Barbara's remarkable traits: she was always best on the first take. In subsequent takes she lost her naturalness and got stiff and forced.

Each day Capra let her do a scene the way she wanted to, watching her carefully. Pleased with her work, he sug-

gested she watch the rushes with him. She said very little
to Capra, but was horrified at what she saw, feeling her
movements were awkward and ugly. The following day
she tried to change and eagerly viewed the rushes again,
but they were terrible.

Capra was well aware of what she was trying to do—
look elegant and beautiful. He told her that by being so
self-conscious she lost her specialness, her complete naturalness. He made her promise never again to look at the
rushes.

And she never did.

The rest of the cast were confused by Capra's decision
to rehearse without her. This had never been done before.
They resented having to do a scene more than once because on the first take the camera focused on Stanwyck
alone. It meant more work for everyone else, but Capra
wasn't concerned about that. He had found a unique actress and the key to her perfection. That was all that mattered.

Capra told her she was not beautiful, and that if she was
going to be a success it was for her acting, not her looks.
She was relieved and afterward was always able to concentrate on being herself.

If Stanwyck did not make friends on the set of *Ladies
of Leisure* because Capra made them work harder than
ordinarily, she was unconcerned since her performance
was a smash and Hollywood at last recognized her talent.
The *New York Times* bannered, "Miss Stanwyck triumphs!" And *Photoplay* magazine raved: "It is a really
fine picture because of the astonishing performance of a
little tap-dancing beauty who has in her the spirit of a
great artist. Her name is Barbara Stanwyck. Go and be
amazed by this Barbara girl."

Ladies of Leisure was one of Stanwyck's greatest films
and many insist she never did better. Hollywood opened
its arms to her and she walked into them like the artist she

was. But success did not change the ex-chorus girl. She was still dedicated, ambitious, and forthright. As for the social butterflies who begged for her at their parties, they were ignored. And those producers and directors who snubbed her had to wait in line.

Frank Fay, however, had not expected to make his wife a star when he pleaded with Frank Capra to watch her screen test. He wanted a minor career for her, but *Ladies of Leisure* had made Barbara one of the most promising actresses in Hollywood. Sadly Frank Fay's theatrical talent did not belong in the movies and he was no longer in demand. Refusing to admit he had made a mistake by moving to California, he nevertheless began to negotiate in 1931 with New York theater owners for his return. Barbara, meanwhile, refused to sign a contract with any major studio, but did agree to nonexclusive contracts with both Columbia and Warner Brothers, a smart decision she made on her own and which set the pattern of independence that was the hallmark of her professional life.

The contract stars were molded by the studios and, although they were undoubtedly the top stars who are still legends today, this was not for Barbara and she was one of the very few who did not need the security of the seven-year standard contract. Fay was upset that she had made deals with two studios because he knew he was through on the West Coast and he couldn't bear to hang around watching her successes at *two* studios. Meanwhile Barbara filmed *Illicit* for Warner Brothers, receiving top billing as "Miss Barbara Stanwyck," which thrilled her more than any other honor possibly could. From then on, she was given this title billing. *Illicit* was a good follow-up to *Ladies of Leisure* and well received.

While studio directors and producers kept her telephone busy, Fay fumed. He made her understand she was his wife first and an actress second. She agreed to that. There was talk of her retiring as soon as he became reestablished in New York. Fay, of course, insisted they were begging him to return and he was, after all, the breadwinner in the family. And the star!

She agreed to that, too.

Whatever Barbara said, however, she was not completely in charge of her own destiny now. Believing Frank was right about a wife's place being at her husband's side, she was sincere in her determination to make the marriage work. Unfortunately a major motion picture studio does not run its business that way, and Columbia refused to let her accompany Frank back to New York even for their second anniversary. She explained in tears to Harry Cohn that Frank was opening at the Palace Theater and was angry enough that she would not be there, but would be mollified if she at least made a brief appearance on their anniversary night. But Cohn flatly refused to let her go because he knew Frank Fay would deliberately delay his wife's return to Hollywood.

She told friends she would retire after her contract with Columbia expired, for love was the most important thing and she didn't want anything to interfere with her marriage to Frank. Her public statements about the primacy of love and marriage were perhaps what she believed in her heart, but nothing could make her live those words. Her career was flourishing, and that soon determined what she would do with her life.

In *Ten Cents a Dance* her Brooklyn accent came in handy as a taxi dancer. One of her best lines was in answer to "What's a guy gotta do to dance with you girls?"

"All ya need is a ticket and some courage!" was her tough response.

During the filming she took a bad fall down some steps which partially paralyzed her, but, tough as ever, she was out of the hospital in one day and back on the set.

The director of *Ten Cents a Dance* was Lionel Barrymore, who was suffering from severe arthritis at the time and taking medication that put him to sleep during most of the filming. Barbara rose above this and made a comment that Barrymore did his best under the circumstances, and that she just had to try a little harder.

Ten Cents a Dance was a cute picture and did nothing to hurt Stanwyck's popularity. Immediately she was sent to Warner's for *Night Nurse* starring a new actor, Clark Gable. The film was a mishmash of crime, drugs, alcohol, and violence, and was popular because of its stars.

There are plenty of punches and violence in *Night Nurse*—Gable involved in most of it. *Hollywood Reporter* gave him a good review but mentioned, "The best things about *Night Nurse* are its title and cast names plus the Misses Stanwyck and Blondell stripping two or three times during the picture." So again Stanwyck was applauded for good work.

She said later that her greatest thrill was her first look at Clark Gable. "Joan Blondell and I were in awe," she sighed. "He was just the kinda guy who made you look at him all the time. Suddenly he became a rage when *A Free Soul* came out with Norma Shearer as his costar. It was Gable who brought the crowds to see *Night Nurse* because the public couldn't get enough of him."

While Stanwyck was on a hectic schedule, Frank Fay returned from New York and appeared in *Bright Lights* and *God's Gift to Women,* both disasters. The reviews were terrible, the moviegoers did not bother with either movie, and Warners was disgusted. Although *Show of Shows* was a smash, it was not Fay who was primarily responsible for the film's acclaim despite his boast that it was. When given an opportunity to prove himself, he flopped in Hollywood and Warners postponed further Fay projects.

Barbara was gliding along nicely and very much in demand, which of course made the situation worse. Fay knew he was finished and survival meant moving back to

New York. He also had to face his wife's blooming career
and how foolish it would be for her to pack her bags
and leave it behind. After three years of marriage, the
Fays had reached a stone wall. Frank began to drink
heavily, putting him in an ugly mood and a raging temper. Now it was he who sat in their big mansion in Brentwood all day waiting for his wife to come home. When
she did, he was already on his way to becoming drunk
and unruly.

It was her turn to understand as he had when he called
Harry Cohn on her behalf. Unfortunately Barbara was
not as powerful as Frank was in 1929. She knew her husband belonged in the theater and, if he were single, could
pick himself up, return to New York, and continue where
he left off. Worse, he had to face the fact that everyone
knew his wife was becoming a big star and he was becoming a has-been and a drunk. Reporters called every
day and rumors were flying. The Fays' neighbors complained to the police about terrible fights. Doors slammed
at all hours, dishes crashed, cars screeched out into the
night. Voices screamed obscenities. When the police arrived, there was nothing they could do except warn the
Fays "to keep it down and stop disturbing the neighbors."

These events made the newspapers. Barbara laughed it
off. When the press called her at home, she said rumors of
divorce were unfounded, and she was making breakfast
for her husband—a sure sign of a happy marriage.

But there were public fights in nightclubs. Fay knocked
her down after accusing her of having too much to drink.
He got into fistfights with men for no apparent reason.
Fay was ready to knock the world down because of his
fallen career, and Barbara was no exception. The private
battles were fierce and he often hit her.

This was the time for Fay to pull himself together. His
career, his image, and his marriage were all in jeopardy.

He desperately loved Barbara and she was very much in love with him. They seemed made for each other. Who would have suspected that the Fay marriage would begin to crumble with violence? Frank had always appeared happy, always doing something important. It didn't matter; he was a man of action, ego, and temperament. But, like Byron Stevens, he was hot-tempered and selfish.

During the roaring battles in the Brentwood mansion, Barbara found salvation working with director Frank Capra again in *The Miracle Woman*, the story of evangelist Aimee Semple McPherson. Stanwyck portrays a phony preacher, but finds her way by the end of the film when she saves the church to the tune of "Onward Christian Soldiers." She was superb. The movie was banned in England, making it more popular in America. *The Miracle Woman* would have been acclaimed anyway.

The higher Stanwyck climbed, the lower Fay sank. Warner Brothers canceled its contract with him in June 1931. When the studio released the information, they graciously said it was "by mutual consent."

Barbara was hounded by the press, and she told another story: "Frank did not like the scripts that were given to him and he has turned down many offers," she said, giving a fair performance. "I am glad that he was able to get out of his contract and can now accept other engagements that have been pending. He did a couple bad films, but so what? The same thing could happen to me. I've been through it."

Naturally reporters wanted to know how the situation was at home.

"Frank prefers that his wife stay home, but he is indirectly responsible for what has happened to me in Hollywood because he wants me to be happy. That's the way it should be when you're in love."

Trying hard to pacify Frank, she did everything to restore some balance in a critically unbalanced relationship.

If she was not succeeding at home, perhaps she could spare Frank's dignity with the public and the press.

After all the denials and all the lies and all the broken dishes, it was just a matter of time before the final showdown and a major decision. Frank was returning to the New York stage and this was final. He expected Barbara to move back to the East Coast with him. She did not refuse, but calmly reminded Frank she was still under contract and how it would look if he were the one responsible for her walking out to be with him. Fay thought that one over, but it did not take him long to come up with a solution.

Barbara was scheduled to work with Frank Capra again in Columbia's *Forbidden*. She did not want to blemish her reputation by ignoring her commitments, but she wanted a vacation. Columbia, however, expected her to report for work immediately.

In July 1931 she called Harry Cohn to tell him she was going to New York with her husband and would not be available for work. She told him, though, that if he wanted her badly enough, he'd have to pay her $50,000 a picture instead of her current $30,000. Cohn's language would shock a sailor even when the producer was in good humor, but what he said to Stanwyck cannot be quoted. When he got nowhere, he finally shouted, "I'll sue you!" And that's what he did.

The movie magazines went wild with articles about how much in love Barbara was with her husband and how she had told Hollywood they would have to wait until Faysie decided his wife could return to films. She was referred to as independent, and the consensus was she had every right to demand the money she deserved. For a while Stanwyck was written up in positive terms until Louella Parsons got into the fray. "Is it possible Frank Fay is being selfish and thinking only of himself?" she wrote. "It seems to me Barbara is making all the sacrifices and this lawsuit is just a means of covering up the real reason for her not reporting for work at Columbia."

Barbara spent August and most of September in New York with Frank until Columbia decided to get even tougher. They obtained an injunction preventing Stanwyck from working for any other studio until she had honored her contract with them. She had lost and in a panic returned to Hollywood. Cohn greeted her personally and said there were no hard feelings. He was delighted to have her back. She lost the case, but Cohn gave her the $50,000 anyway!

In the tearjerker *Forbidden* with Adolphe Menjou, a remake of Fannie Hurst's *Back Street*, Barbara maintained her fine acting. Moviegoers loved it. The *New York World-Telegram* said she was "one of the few really fine and intelligent actresses on the screen." According to London's *Film Weekly*, "Miss Stanwyck's emotional scenes with Menjou show that she can hold her own with any actress on the screen today."

She could not, however, hold her own on a horse in *Forbidden* and was thrown to the sand. She insisted on finishing the scene before going to the hospital. Terrified of horses, Stanwyck always used a double in these early days as an actress; she was thrown when the horse was standing still but then reared when the lights blazed in its eyes. She remained home for several days with two sprained legs.

After completing *Forbidden* Stanwyck returned to New York and shocked her fans and Hollywood by appearing with Fay at the Palace. Part of their act was strictly slapstick. All right, the press said, she was his wife and had been a chorus girl and flapper. But when she did scenes from *Ladies of Leisure, The Miracle Woman,* and *Forbidden* on the Palace stage, it was not acceptable as class or in good taste to "advertise" her movies on the legitimate stage, far superior to movies. She did draw the crowds, of course, despite Fay's taking all the credit "because New York had missed him so desperately when Hollywood begged for his talent." Underneath his bragging, pangs of jealousy were clouding his ability to think straight. Not only was he jealous of Barbara's popularity, he was now jealous of other men and would not allow her out of his sight. When he was on stage alone, she was instructed to watch from the wings so he knew where she was. Everyone connected with the show at the Palace knew Fay was straining to keep his name in lights. And Stanwyck was straining to keep her name off the marquee. Louella Parsons hinted in her columns that all those concerned wondered how many more sacrifices Barbara would make for her husband, but Barbara claimed, "I would remain with Frank at the Palace Theater indefinitely were it not for my film commitments in Hollywood."

Returning to the cameras in Columbia's *Shopworn* was not a happy event following better films and the not-so-happy stay in New York with her possessive husband. One of her costars in *Shopworn* said: "Barbara was not happy. The picture was low budget and the script quite shallow. It was one of those films that, regardless of how much effort she put into it, would not be worthy. I think she might have overcome this if she had not been unhappy in general."

The Times of London said the movie was dull and characterless, but Stanwyck "does what she can with a thankless part," and the *New York Herald Tribune* praised her: "There is something about the simple, straightforward sincerity of Miss Stanwyck which makes almost everything she does upon the stage or screen seem credible and rather poignant. [But] in such antique surroundings, the work of the star is virtually ineffective."

Critical acclaim continued in Warner Brothers' *So Big*, based on Edna Ferber's best-selling novel. The *New York*

World-Telegram wrote: "By her performance in *So Big*
Barbara Stanwyck definitely establishes herself with this
writer as being a brilliant emotional actress. No matter
what one may think about the picture, the final conviction
of anyone who sees Miss Stanwyck's Selma Peake will be
that she herself contributes a fine and stirring performance, making of it a characterization which is direct and
eloquent all the way."

Stanwyck was considered the third most popular actress in America.

In *The Purchase Price* for Warners with George Brent,
Barbara gave her usual fine performance. Stanwyck's popularity at the box office kept her name in the newspapers
and fan magazines, but she tried to avoid comment on her
marriage, as did Warners and Columbia. Fay's booking at
the Palace was over and he returned to Hollywood to little
enthusiasm: the town had labeled him a failure. His heavy
drinking remained a problem. He and Barbara loved the
nightclub scene, but Fay made sure she was not out of his
sight despite the fact that he ignored her. He was trying
very hard to convince the movie colony that he was the
star in the family and Barbara was merely fulfilling her
contract. After that, she would give up her career to be a
full-time wife to the great Frank Fay. In the meantime
New York and Broadway clamored for him.

Friends watched Fay's excessive drinking and worried
because Barbara was keeping up with him in public. He
blamed her for disagreements and said it was her fault
they began to lose friends. Because of their excessive behavior, slowly they were being excluded from parties and
not asked to join the usual crowd at nightclubs.

This didn't faze Barbara because she was busy studying scripts in the evenings and on her days off. But Fay
was losing all of his important contacts, such as they were,
and he needed social exposure. He would not, however,
admit it was his fault that they were omitted from the
guest lists.

Fay was arrested for drunken driving and hit-and-run when his car hit another on Beverly Boulevard, but charges were dropped when witnesses refused to testify.

Barbara did not take this lightly, but she was more concerned for her husband's well-being than any adverse publicity. Extremely nervous and upset, she tried to give her all to Frank without giving up her career. This was not possible, and it was the second—and last—time she would make this mistake. As a disciplined and dedicated woman, her personality required every ounce of energy and minute of her time to be devoted to her career as an actress. Her rushing off with Fay to New York cost Barbara nothing.

She agreed to help Frank with their own stage production entitled *Tattle Tales* and invested $125,000 of her own money. But before the production could be realized, Barbara had to complete four films in rapid succession. Meanwhile, Frank was busy writing and arranging for another big New York comeback, and life for the Fays seemed a little bit brighter.

With Frank Capra as the director of her last film for Columbia, *The Bitter Tea of General Yen*, Barbara portrayed the American mistress of a Chinese warlord. This picture was Stanwyck's most unusual and Hollywood wondered why she bothered to make it. So did her fans. The *New York Times* said she failed to be convincing: "Her powerful voice is scarcely what is needed to carry out the theme of this tale of romance between a handsome Chinese general and a lovely American missionary."

This was Stanwyck's only "art" film and Capra was pushing for an Academy Award. He claims it lost money because it was banned in England, yet the same ban did not affect *The Miracle Woman*, and, if anything, boosted sales.

Now under exclusive contract to Warner Brothers, Stanwyck did *Ladies They Talk About* in which she played the wisecracking tough broad that was so like

Stanwyck in her best roles. The movie was finished in only twenty-four days and was greeted by mixed reviews, but generally the critics agreed there was honesty to her performance.

Warners decided Barbara Stanwyck needed a glamorous role. "I guess everyone in Hollywood is glamorous but me," she said. "So I accepted a role in *Baby Face* strictly for glamour and hated it."

Ever in My Heart followed quickly and Stanwyck was much happier with tragedy as her theme. The *New York World-Telegram* wrote: "Barbara Stanwyck demonstrates that she is one of the first and the very first actresses among the more exalted leading ladies in Hollywood. She gives a fine, dignified performance. . . . It is one of the most searching and authentic characterizations [she] has yet offered."

With four fairly successful movies behind her, Stanwyck was determined to help her husband. Broke and unhappy, Frank was fighting desperately. The country was struggling through the depression, and vaudeville had bowed to the booming movie industry. The theaters that once featured live stage shows were being converted into movie theaters. With Barbara's money, they produced *Tattle Tales*, a stage revue that played the major cities gearing up for the Broadhurst Theater on June 11, 1933.

One critic sums up the disaster: "Frank Fay does not know where to draw the line. I like Fay very much and I always have, but he refuses to believe that there is a difference between acting and being Frank Fay! He will be what nature made him, let the chips fall where they may. He is a problem child. Now at the 44th Street Theater he is producing a vaudeville show and he is one of its three stars. The trouble with it is he thinks he owns it! . . . There is no one there to stop him from doing what he wants. So he does everything and anything he wants all evening. If he is funny for a minute he jumps to the childish conclusion that if he keeps going for ten minutes he will be ten times as funny. He never knows when to go home.

"There ought to be a commission appointed for the conservation of Frank Fay. Or he could go to a good psychiatrist and be turned into an artist with hardly any trouble at all.

"I hate to see Frank Fay go to waste. He is too good."

But, as it happens for all vaudevillians, the spotlight grew dim and Fay thought he could out-perform the light bulbs. Instead they burst in his face; after only twenty-eight days, *Tattle Tales* closed and Barbara lost almost $200,000. She was also losing her battle to keep her marriage together as Frank lost his battle with the bottle. When they returned to their Brentwood mansion, Barbara had only one hope left.

She and Frank adopted a ten-month-old baby and christened him Dion Anthony Fay. If Barbara thought a baby could mend the mounting troubles, she should have recalled her own childhood when Byron became more restless with the birth of each son and daughter, finally leaving them to fend for themselves. If she thought her dedication as a foster mother would be any different from the many who took her in as orphaned Ruby Stevens, she should have thought again. Or if she expected to be like her own mother, Catherine, a housewife with loving and maternal instincts who cared especially about children, Barbara might have given this major step more consideration.

But children meant a good image, and posing with Dion for publicity could only boost her femininity.

Hollywood insiders were not fooled. They were disappointed that the Fays had even thought of bringing a child into a household of bitter fights, drunken sprees, and a disoriented life-style. Neither Barbara nor Frank spoke about wanting children before. More surprising was that they were allowed to adopt a child, since they would not have been considered fit parents if anyone had taken time to investigate them thoroughly.

Dion got to know his nanny very well because Barbara was much too busy with her career. She was at the studio all day and, if she wasn't learning her lines in the evening, she and Frank were nightclubbing.

Friends wondered why a child had to suffer silently, as they also wondered about Joan Crawford and her daughter. Of course, friends are ordinarily people who say what others are afraid to, but in Hollywood they are most likely to sit back, observe, and hope that what they see isn't the way it will always be.

Barbara was too clever a woman not to know about the gossip over her failing marriage and the little baby who did not belong.

"Sometimes it seems that Hollywood does not want people to be happy," she said in an interview. "Why don't they leave us alone? We're going to be happy in spite of everyone. They are determined that nobody has a private life that is immune from chatter and scandal. You know that people are watching you all the time, looking for the slightest thing to gossip about and, if they don't find it, they make it up. That is why Frank and I go out with only close friends. All we ask is to be allowed to live in peace, but some people resent that. Well, they'll just have to go on resenting!"

Reporters doubted there was resentment. No one envied Barbara's marriage or resented the big mansion that was void of dinner parties and friends. No one in Hollywood was jealous of Barbara's life beyond the studio gates. Fay was still beating her up and it was no secret, and he was still getting into fist fights. If Barbara interfered, he gave her one to the jaw, too. The joke was, "The only one Fay can beat up without getting knocked out cold is his wife!"

The few friends who came to visit the Fays in Brentwood said they rarely, if ever, saw Dion. He was locked in his room with his nanny. Apparently he was not allowed out because once in a drunken rage Fay threw the baby in the swimming pool. "Unfortunately," a neighbor said, "the child did not calm things down in that house. It got worse and the police were summoned as often as ever. If they were normal parents, the baby would have been taken away from them long ago."

The Fays were no longer interested in entertaining. Barbara was never one to care about house guests either for an hour or overnight, and Frank was rarely sober. The house was laden with antiques and silverware, and friends said they lived lavishly. Barbara claimed to want no part of Hollywood society, after being snubbed so badly when she could not get a job, and the upper classes did not beg for her company. She was accepted as a fine actress and her ability to get along with her coworkers was beyond question. But when the cameras dimmed, there were few invitations to fashionable gatherings.

Frank's heavy drinking and profanity rubbed off on his wife. But, unlike Broadway's code, Hollywood's was strict on the surface. Its glowing stars lived by two standards—proper on the outside and a little impropriety behind closed doors as long as it remained private.

The Fays lacked the sophistication and class of the beautiful Hollywood people. They could have pretended if they chose to, but making the right impression was a waste of time to them. They were what they were.

One night at the Trocadero nightclub in Hollywood Frank accused his wife of being drunk and landed a wallop to her chin that sent her to the floor. After a brief parting, Barbara was the first to break the silence with a letter:

> No need to tell you that I felt blue when you left. I can't stand your being unhappy in any way at all. Whatever you

want to do I am with you 100 percent only I do not want you to sacrifice yourself in any way. I can live any place or go anywhere with you.

I love you just as much as it is possible for a woman to love a man. If I were born with anything fine in me, and I choose to think I was from what I know of my father and mother, you have brought that fineness to the surface.

I cannot imagine life without you and I am not being melodramatic.

I probably do not give you that impression at any time—that of not being able to imagine life without you, I mean. However, that is due to my lack of education and not being able to express myself clearly in speech.

I can write it, however. You are always right about everything so you must be right about what you want to do. Please, Frank, love me—whatever you do. And wherever you go, take me. For there I shall be content.

While Dion Fay got to know his nanny and wondered what the mother who adopted him was like, she was fighting for better scripts.

"I worry day and night over stories," she sighed. "Right now I'm in the doghouse at the studio because I turned down several stories they wanted me to do which I didn't feel were right for me.

"Then they wanted me to do *British Agent* with Leslie Howard. I read the book twice because I found it so absorbing, but it's a man's story. Howard was made to order for the part, but I turned it down because I saw no reason why I should play second fiddle to anyone. I've worked too hard to get to the top to give up top billing for no good reason. I don't mean the actual billing because that's unimportant. I mean the top spot in the picture. In a few years, I suppose, I'll have to resign myself to supporting parts—we all come to that eventually—but I don't feel that I have come to that point yet."

Gambling Lady with Joel McCrea was a good film, but *A Lost Lady* and *The Secret Bride* were boring films. She completed her contract with Warner Brothers in *The Woman in Red* and Barbara was free of obligations. Unlike her, she took a six-month vacation, but only to negotiate with other studios and to find an agent to help her handle business affairs.

Zeppo Marx, one of the famous Marx Brothers and an extremely successful agent in Hollywood, not only was Barbara's agent but one of her closest friends. She preferred being a freelance actress and Marx saw nothing wrong with that. He and his wife, Marion, soon would be responsible for the turning point in Barbara's personal life.

Red Salute with Robert Young was not a successful film. Released by United Artists, it was Barbara's first comedy and, although primarily a dramatic actress, she had an innate flare for humor, as she proved later in her career.

Robert Young said that the best part of *Red Salute* was making it. He always arrived on the set early—but found Barbara already there. So then he came in a little earlier, she was there before him again. Then he came still earlier; she was there. It turned out she was watching him and made sure she got there first. This was Barbara's way of having fun!

Despite the bad films she was making, Stanwyck was nonetheless recognized as a big star and critics praised her performances despite poor scripts. She always managed to make the films better than they deserved to be, and she always got loyal support from her many fans around the country and in Europe.

Barbara could always "hold a script together," but after almost ruining her career by taking off to New York with *Tattle Tales* and ruining her health by putting up with Fay's physical and mental abuse, as well as adopting a baby boy, she could not keep her marriage together. It should have ended long ago, but by hanging on she indirectly destroyed Fay's career by refusing to move back to New York with him, lost a great deal of money—and gained a child that she was too busy to love.

After a brief fight around their swimming pool, Frank hit Barbara yet again, this time because she had attended a burlesque show. She hit the ground and sadly Dion was a witness. Barbara told Frank she wanted a divorce and this time she meant it.

The Stanwyck personality that we've known for so many years is far removed from that of the twenty-seven-year-old ex-chorus girl weeping for her husband's return. He was, despite his drunken brawls and waning career, the stronger of the two; although she paid the bills, he was always the man of the house.

She struggled with her sanity but never doubted her love for Fay. It would take awhile before she had enough faith in herself to stand alone and put the past in perspective. She realized he had been greatly responsible for her success in Hollywood, and although she was the one who never forgot an injustice, neither did she forget a favor or helping hand.

Oddly Frank might have regained his professional status had she not sought him out after each separation. California is a long way from New York and the movie industry even further from the Broadway stage. Had he returned to what was left of vaudeville, his career would not have remained moribund.

In a letter dated November 17, 1934, she wrote to him on his birthday:

Dear Kid,
I haven't diamonds, no watch, no nothing. I feel rather funny not sending you anything, but it just has to be. And so, Frank, all I have to give you today is my prayers that all go well for you. And whatever you do shall be right, and that God will keep your path well-lighted so that you will never hurt yourself. God bless you and spare you.

BarBara

Early in 1935 she told the press, "I'll never divorce Frank Fay! Never! You can gossip all you want, but if I can't stay married, I'll get out of pictures!"

But at the Brown Derby restaurant Fay got drunk and attacked Eddie Mannix, general studio manager of Metro-Goldwyn-Mayer. There was no studio behind Barbara to protect her this time and the story made headlines. Hollywood remembers this incident very well. Fay's abusive, drunken sprees and his brutality would have to end sometime before someone got killed—probably his wife. Yet through this whole mess, this whole ugly charade, Fay continued to tell the press that he was the star in the family and that Barbara was going to retire. Reporters could recite his speeches by heart.

In August 1935 Barbara left Frank, and this time it was the end. She left so quickly that she did not take her choice antiques and silver which she had been collecting over the years. Frank got possession of the Brentwood mansion, and Barbara was indifferent.

She took Dion, of course, and together with nanny they moved into a ranch in the Northridge section on the far corner of the San Fernando Valley near her friends, Zeppo and Marion Marx. Here she established Marwyck [Marx–Stanwyck] Ranch to breed thoroughbred horses on 140 acres of land.

The Brentwood house was eventually sold to Jack Oakie for $80,000. Barbara got custody of Dion and filed for divorce based on mental cruelty. She and Frank signed a predivorce settlement on December 31, 1935, and he was allowed to visit his son twice a week.

Three

While Barbara was waiting for her lawyers to settle her divorce affairs, she accepted the role of *Annie Oakley*, without a doubt one of her best performances. Her own personality matched the character of Annie—spunky, determined, tough, and straightforward. It was also Barbara's first Western—the first of many she would make in her career. Preston Foster was her costar, but this was Stanwyck's film and the critics went wild.

The *New York World-Telegram:* "The talented and attractive Barbara Stanwyck gives by far the best performance of her career. From the moment she appears . . . as the gawky little country girl of humble origin . . . to the time when she is acclaimed by the crowned heads of Europe for her unexcelled marksmanship, Miss Stanwyck plays the role with such commendable restraint and with such feeling for the character that she almost becomes Annie Oakley."

The *New York Sun:* "Barbara Stanwyck's presence, as well as an excellent script, pulls the picture definitely out of the 'for the children only' class. Her curious quality of

sincerity, strikingly rare on the screen, gives the story un-
expected tenderness and dignity. A Western with Miss
Stanwyck playing the shy, girlish young queen of the
shooting range becomes a super-Western indeed."

The *New York Times:* "Barbara Stanwyck is splendid
in the title role; this is her most striking performance in a
long time."

Annie Oakley was an RKO picture and the studio
wanted Stanwyck to sign with them. She would not give
them an exclusive, but did sign for future work. Twentieth Century–Fox also negotiated with her. Stanwyck
did not have to brag that over five studios were willing to
give her what she wanted.

But despite this adulation, her first assignment with
Twentieth Century–Fox was not good. *A Message to
García,* with Wallace Beery and John Boles, was somewhat similar to her worst in 1930, *Mexicali Rose,* and was
all wrong for her. Again her Spanish mixed with the
Brooklyn accent was a joke. Why she was given—and accepted—second billing to Wallace Beery is still a mystery.
Just about everything about *A Message to García* was
terrible, although Boles and Beery were praised in the reviews. But the critics did not know how to respond to
Stanwyck. The *New York Evening Post* said, "It bothers
us that Barbara, cast as the Cuban Senorita, should talk
perfect Brooklyn."

What did Stanwyck have to say about the farce? "I
enjoy working."

The Bride Walks Out with Gene Raymond and Robert
Young gave Barbara another chance at high comedy, but
the film was only fair.

Stanwyck, who had gained recognition for the ability to
hold an audience's attention through her expressions of
sorrow and tragedy, had easily made even the skeptics
weep. She had yet to loosen up in light comedy, but she
would, of course, become highly skilled at it.

According to her former press agent and friend Helen
Ferguson, Barbara patterned her walk on the panther's
movements. "She spent hours at the zoo," Miss Ferguson
said, "pacing back and forth with the panthers, who
walked slowly, determinately, lightfooted, and in stride.
Barbara wanted a walk of distinction, not sensuality.
There was no trace of hips swinging or the popular wig-
gle. She was too much aware of herself and never gave in
to attracting attention that way."

She was self-made and individualistic.

Her friend Joan Crawford has aptly described their
struggles for stardom: "Barbara and I were very much
alike. Our backgrounds were very similar. We were hard-
working hoofers who didn't expect much more in life. We
clawed our way to the top. We were not ashamed of what
we were, but finding ourselves dramatic actresses meant
looking and appearing like the actresses who were
groomed for stardom. We were, of course, self-conscious
for a long time. The likes of such great ladies as Greer
Garson and Norma Shearer could make any ex-hoofer
terrified of not being good enough."

And with the feeling of not being good enough to hold
her marriage together, Barbara Stanwyck walked into divorce court. She told the judge that there had been "too
many women attracted to Fay and he enjoyed it too
much." She told reporters, "I hated to have to do this, but
it seems the only salvation for both of us. Frank is better
off alone and so am I. I want our divorce to be free of bitterness."

She was awarded custody of Dion, but there were
many battles in court to come.

Frank Fay forged ahead with nightclub engagements.
"I should've done this before," he said, "but I believed a
husband and wife should live together. Barbara made it
big in Hollywood. I need the live audience—the kick from
laughs and applause—the reaction type thing. I helped

when I had pull at Warners and they gave her a break. I'm not sorry I did that, but who the hell could've predicted the outcome. There was no way out in the end except divorce."

Allowed visitation rights two days a week, Fay was not always in California, but called Dion as often as possible. "For a hundred bucks a call," he complained, "all I got was 'Hello, Daddy' and dead air! When I got to town, I was told I wasn't allowed to see my son."

Fay's lawyers contacted Stanwyck's attorneys, who claimed that Frank was always drunk and therefore dangerous to the welfare of the child. The bickering continued, but Fay was barred from the ranch. When the judge ordered her to allow him in to see Dion, she refused and was summoned to court to give valid reasons why Fay could not exercise his rights under the divorce agreement.

While the complicated case was being prepared by both sides, Barbara began dating occasionally. She was seen with George Brent, who escorted many of his leading ladies to the theater and other glittering events. Her brother, Byron, moved to Hollywood and was seen with his sister on special occasions. Byron was the mystery man for a while until his identity became known.

Although Barbara looked content, she was carrying a torch for Fay. There was no turning back, but the hopelessness of it all was heartbreaking. Being alone again was the deepest hurt of all. Regardless of the ending, she and Fay were in many ways made for each other. They were the same breed, and finding one like him in Hollywood was unlikely.

Stanwyck was not a quitter and she considered divorce a sign that either or both gave up without trying a little bit harder. She was still in love with Fay when she walked into divorce court and her previous attempts to reconcile were desperate, but sincere. Her letters indicate that clearly.

A close pal confided that the one thing Barbara did not do was give up drinking. "It's possible that Frank might have drank less. She invested her money, which was no big deal because she had plenty of that. She invested her time to suit her own movie schedule. But she did not invest a few months of complete sobriety on both sides— time away from Broadway and Hollywood, the parties and the bars, to help him kick alcoholism."

Alone, however, she found contentment at Marwyck, thirty miles from Hollywood. An old friend, Buck Mack, took care of the ranch for her and watched over the thoroughbreds when she was away. This was her first experience at country living.

"I miss the city," she told reporters, "but right now I don't want people staring at me. I need a peaceful home for me and my son. If my ranch appears typical of Hollywood, it wasn't meant to be that way. Hollywood represents hard work, not glamour. It also represents the ability to live comfortably. Right now I have everything I want. It's hard work that gets you anywhere. I have given up wishing."

But in the fall of 1936, every girl's wish came true for Barbara Stanwyck. Every girl's dream walked into her arms. Without looking, searching, or trying, little Ruby Stevens from Brooklyn found Camelot.

Zeppo and Marion Marx invited Barbara for dinner at the famous nightclub Trocadero. They wanted her to meet someone. When she arrived there was no one sitting at the reserved table other than matinee idol Robert Taylor, whom she recognized. They chatted politely, but each time the door opened, she looked around. Feeling awkward, he asked her to dance.

"I can't right now," she said, "Zeppo wants me to meet someone—a Mr. Artique."

"Mr. Artique?" Taylor frowned. "Never heard of him. What's the first name?"

"I don't know," she said, keeping her eye on the door.

He found himself also looking around for a single gentleman. "That's a peculiar name, isn't it?" he asked.

"Maybe I'm not pronouncing it right, but it's close enough."

"Artique . . . Artique . . . " he repeated over and over. Then he laughed. "That's me! R.T. Get it? R.T.?"

Taylor yelped like a puppy and was, undoubtedly, more excited about the misunderstanding than she was. Barbara, downhearted over Fay, was not interested in romance, especially from a twenty-five-year-old puppy. Taylor, despite his enthusiasm over his date with the distinguished Miss Barbara Stanwyck was still in love with actress Irene Hervey. But, watching them on the dance floor that night, no one would believe the torches they carried for the two absent people.

Barbara thought his young and spirited attitude refreshing. Her down-to-earth humor and carefree laughter made Taylor feel at ease. They shared similar evenings with Marion and Zeppo, but neither Bob nor Barbara wanted to be seen together in public. She was involved in a messy court action with Fay, and he had his obligation to MGM as a single, unattached male performer who dated young starlets. Barbara Stanwyck was not exactly what his studio had in mind. She was four years older than Taylor, divorced, and not the type of girl suited to his image at all.

Robert Taylor was born Spangler Arlington Brugh in Filley, Nebraska, on August 5, 1911. He was raised in Beatrice, Nebraska. His father was a doctor and his mother a sickly woman who was not expected to live through childbirth.

Arly, as he was known, wanted to be a concert cellist. He rode his horse Gypsy to the nearby town of Crete, where Professor Gray taught at Doane College. "Profes-

sor Gray was my inspiration," Taylor said. "I enrolled
at Doane to be with him. My parents gave me an old car
that barely made it. But I remember the day the professor
told me he was accepting a teaching job at Pomona College in Claremont, California, and my whole world fell
apart."

Looking back, Taylor doesn't know how he convinced
his parents to let him transfer to Pomona. "It was a miracle," he said, "and even more astounding that my old car
made it all the way to California!"

Gray was very strict and expressed his disappointment
when Arly took up debating, which led to his being asked
to join the Drama Club. Gray said this was not dedication
to the cello, but Arly said he could cram everything in.
He appeared in several college plays, but it was his role as
Captain Stanhope in R. C. Sherriff's powerful *Journey's
End* that caught the eye of Ben Piazza, talent scout for
MGM. Taylor took a screen test—"It was awful. I could
see they were disappointed." He was told to come back
after he graduated from college.

His father and mother attended graduation. Arly told
the doctor about the screen test. "They told me to come
back," he scowled, "but you know what that means."

"I'd say it means to come back and try again!" his father
said.

MGM did not remember Spangler Arlington Brugh,
but they put him in the acting school until, nine months
later, they signed him to a seven-year contract paying
only thirty-five dollars a week—the lowest-paid actor or
actress in the history of Hollywood.

Dr. Brugh died before his son got the job, but Taylor
never forgot his father's words: *Come back and try again!*

His mother, Ruth, moved to Hollywood and lived with
Arly. They had no money, and thirty-five dollars a
week—even in 1934—did not go far.

Louis B. Mayer, head of MGM, changed Arly's name to
Robert Taylor. "This was a letdown," Taylor confessed.

"After having a distinguished name like Spangler Arlington Brugh, who could accept such a common name—Robert Taylor?"

But with a salary he couldn't live on and a name he hated, he stuck it out at MGM. In his eighth film, *Magnificent Obsession* with Irene Dunne, Robert Taylor, regardless of his name, became a star and was earning $750 a week.

Although success did not come overnight to the innocent young man from Nebraska, it seemed that way. Without an inflated ego and unaware of his handsome—almost beautiful—face Taylor was unsophisticated, trusting, and willing to learn. He had all the traits MGM cherished. Louis B. Mayer told Taylor what and what not to do, and Taylor obeyed because MGM promised to make him a star—and they did. When he dated the older divorcée Virginia Bruce, MGM shook their heads. Exit Miss Bruce.

She wasn't really Taylor's type, anyway. But Irene Hervey, MGM starlet, was, and they fell in love. After a short engagement MGM still refused to allow Taylor to marry because of his single and eligible image. Irene, who was not interested in a career, knew better than to wait for Bob's wedding band. Instead she married singer Allen Jones and became the mother of Jack Jones.

Taylor was deeply hurt. Mayer, who had become Bob's surrogate father, helped Taylor through hard times, but he might have given Irene Hervey more hope if he had realized that the romantic involvement Taylor would later face would be far more complicated.

Rather than retaliate and nurse his wounds by dating other women, Taylor stayed by himself and went to parties alone. He had no desire to become involved for a long time until, that is, he met the "Queen."

If it is true that opposites attract, Taylor and Stanwyck are the classic example. He was still a kid, while Barbara

had never really been a child. He was a top box-office attraction, but lacked the well-developed genuine talent she
had. Taylor was well educated. Barbara was not. He was
soft. She was hard. He would always be a country boy,
but she could breathe freely only in the city. He liked the
femininity of frilly blouses, soft colors, and flouncy skirts.
She liked tailored clothes, suits, sports outfits, and slacks
made out of men's materials. He liked to treat a woman
like a lady. Barbara lit her own cigarettes and opened her
own doors. Bob was discreet, she was brutally frank and
made remarks about herself before anyone else could get
around to it.

He loved to hunt. She thought it was cruel. He loved
guns. She was terrified of them. He loved dogs, but she
was allergic to them.

Taylor could hold his liquor, but did not care for
it. Barbara was a good drinker and liked to put her feet
up on the table chatting in her characteristic New York
accent.

He was an inexperienced and unsophisticated lover.

Barbara had been around.

Taylor's understatement to the press was that, "Miss
Stanwyck is not the sort of woman I would have met in
Nebraska."

Reporters got a snicker out of that one.

Years later Taylor admitted, "Barbara taught me
everything I knew."

As for MGM? They were not concerned, quite yet.
They reversed their outlook on a professional basis and
decided to exploit Taylor's close relationship with a
woman. They asked Barbara to costar with Taylor in *His
Brother's Wife*. It was obvious to everyone on the set that
their love scenes were sincere. Every day they lunched together in her dressing room or his, and he never let her
begin the day without a basket of flowers.

The critics were favorable. The press did not think

Taylor was the type to portray a lab scientist, exposed to fever-bearing ticks, but his enormous popularity would outweigh unfavorable comments.

The *New York Times* summed up the critical consensus: "Whatever else may be said of it, there is no disputing the formulary perfection of the Capitol Theater's latest gift from MGM. Incredibly romantic, glossily produced, expertly directed and peopled by the sort of players most often encountered on the covers of the fan magazines, *His Brother's Wife*—even to its title—has been so astutely aimed at the box office that we can but stiffen resignedly and wait for the marker to cry bull's-eye. A triumph of machine-made art, it is a picture that will succeed no matter how we, in our ivory tower, rail against it for its romantic absurdity."

But Taylor was more excited with *Private Number*. Loretta Young was his costar, but he got top billing. He had never seen his name in lights above all the others. Taylor was impressed while he and Barbara stood across the street from Grauman's Chinese Theater gazing up at the marquee. "Gosh, look at that!" he exclaimed.

Barbara said, "Don't let it go to your head. Loretta has been working for years to get her name up there. You've been at it a short time. The trick is to keep it there!"

Taylor said he grew up a little bit that night. No one had put him down before. "She was right," he confessed, "and it was the best advice I ever had. I never forgot it."

Louis B. Mayer knew that Bob's mother, Ruth, was a nuisance rather than a supportive figure. She interfered with his normal growth as an individual, and, worse, she confronted him continually with the sins and evils in Hollywood. Mayer hoped that Barbara would be a substitute for the confidence and support Bob required. Stanwyck was a professional—a dedicated actress who was prompt and astute with her lines. If this rubbed off on Taylor, MGM could only benefit.

Mayer doubted the relationship would amount to anything. Stanwyck was four years older than Bob and she
had a young son. And besides, they were so different. If
Ruth Brugh did not intervene by either becoming critically ill or crying her son out of anything lasting, MGM
would set the ground rules as they had with Irene Hervey. Marriage or stardom, it was as simple as that.

Barbara was wise by not tampering with Mayer's de-
mands or decisions. She was used to the waiting game and
much too busy with her own career.

At RKO she filmed *The Plough and the Stars* working
again with Preston Foster. Unfortunately the film,
directed by John Ford, was not released before Ford left
for Hawaii on vacation and while he was gone RKO exec-
utives changed their minds about his version of a married
couple involved in the 1916 Easter rebellion in Dublin.
RKO thought if they portrayed unmarried lovers, it
would lend more romance to the script. But in filming the
revised version, Stanwyck lacked sparkle because she disliked the new story line, the master Ford was not di-
recting—and she was never as effective redoing film
footage.

Banjo on My Knee with Joel McCrea at Twentieth
Century–Fox was a light comedy and Barbara made her
singing debut with Tony Martin and Buddy Ebsen. The
director John Cromwell, who said the movie was for
laughs and little else, wanted Stanwyck for the part of the
bride deserted on her wedding day and forced to entertain
for a living. "She had the right quality," he said, "because
of her ability to be spunky and sweet at the same time."

Critics enjoyed reviewing her singing voice, which they
all agreed was deep and throaty. Aside from knowing she
could sing as well as act, Stanwyck's reaction to warbling
"Where the Lazy River Goes By" was, "By the river they
should have cared less!"

She and Joel McCrea were featured together again in

the first Dr. Kildare movie *Internes Can't Take Money*, a
Paramount release. Director Alfred Santell and the cast
discovered an amazing side of Barbara: not only did she
know her lines for the entire movie, she knew everyone
else's as well. She knew their set movements and entrances and exits, whether she was in the scene or not.
Barbara explained this was a result of her stage training.
"I have to know everything from the very start," she said.
"This makes me flexible, too. Regardless of what scene we
are filming out of sequence, I know everything that has or
is supposed to happen. If I memorized it day by day, I
would have no concept of what or who my character is
and what is going to happen to her as well as to the
others."

In 1937 Stanwyck and Taylor were seen together often.
Then suddenly he would appear at a party alone and she
somewhere else without him. Sometimes they dated
others. With Taylor, she remained in the background,
claiming it was his turn to enjoy the attention and admiration of the mobs of fans who always gathered wherever he was. She would relax and observe the stampede.

The attempt to hide their affair finally came to an end.
As Barbara's press agent, Helen Ferguson, explains it:
"Everyone in Hollywood knew about them, but there was
a code of honor that even included the fan magazines. Bob
was a movie idol and adored by women all over the world.
MGM did not want him involved. Barbara had just divorced Frank Fay and was about to go to court over custody of their adopted son. But aside from the obvious
reasons, Bob and Barbara did not know how they felt
about each other. When they realized it was foolish to
date others, which proved nothing, they became a steady
couple."

Again MGM decided to exploit their relationship by
loaning Taylor to Twentieth Century–Fox for *This Is My
Affair* with Stanwyck. The title was sensational, consid-

ering the circumstances, and the public was anxious to see
the two unmarried lovers having "an affair" on the screen.
But they were disappointed. It was far from a romantic
movie; rather, it was the story of an undercover agent
(Taylor) who tries to crush a wave of bank robberies in
the Middle West during Theodore Roosevelt's presi-
dency. Barbara played a music hall entertainer and again
she did her own singing. The cast and crew said it was a
relaxing and romantic experience working with Bob and
Barbara because their happiness rubbed off on everyone.
She remained on the set during his scenes and he did the
same. She was a bit concerned singing "I Hum a Waltz"
with Taylor sitting in the middle of the orchestra. She
thought it was cute, but lost her concentration. She
stopped singing and shook her head, "How can I get
through this song with you looking at me that way!" she
laughed. "Sit somewhere else!"

"It was all in fun," a coworker said. "Taylor had a habit
of trying to hide his gorgeous face on many movie sets
just to observe, but someone always spotted him. In Barbara's case, it was different. No one else could have forced
her to stop in the middle of a performance whether it was
acting or singing. He was like a little boy."

Though not what the housewives wanted to see, they
did get enough romance, and *This Is My Affair* was a hit.
The critics said Taylor made love to Stanwyck "persua-
sively."

Taylor had just completed *Camille* with Greta Garbo
and *Personal Property* with Jean Harlow, making him the
hottest male star in Hollywood. But his nickname was
Pretty Boy and rumors spread that he was a homosexual—one reason MGM permitted the Taylor–Stanwyck
romance. Taylor was overwhelmed by the type of publicity he was getting. The press harassed him. In one sponta-
neous interview he snarled, "Ask me anything except
about Barbara Stanwyck or if I have hair on my chest!"

Taylor went to Mayer. "I don't get to see much of my fan mail," he complained. "And I know why. They don't think I'm a man!"

"Have I ever let you down, son?" Mayer asked.

"No, sir, but don't you think my image is all wrong?"

"The women love you, Bob. The male public is jealous and you allow reporters to upset you."

"They can say anything they want," Taylor exclaimed, "but not insinuate I'm a homosexual."

"After *Broadway Melody of 1938*, I have a surprise for you. Be patient."

Barbara was sympathetic. She had tried to give him confidence when he faced the great Garbo in *Camille*. Wearing makeup including lipstick upset Taylor. She explained that the part of Armand called for it and that he should just "roll with the punches."

Taylor said Barbara rarely, if ever, helped him with his roles. He was a star and she was an actress. This was accepted from the beginning and neither pretended it was any different. He would try hard to improve his acting over the years, but was guided for a quarter of a century by MGM. Barbara gave him confidence and the urge to go on when the pressure was on. There was little she could do about the "pansy" and "queer" stigma he suffered through, but Taylor said: "One night we went for a drive to the beach and just sat there in silence. Barbara was crying and I had never seen her show such emotion before. She considers it a weakness to give into every mood, but if going through things gives one Barbara's tolerance and appreciation, I wish it could have happened to me. I am awed at what has happened to her. She practically brought up herself. I don't think she could teach anyone that! It took me a long time to realize I could not be like Barbara. She had a rare kind of sympathy. Instead of feeling sorry for someone she told them to get up and get

going. If anyone understood, it was her, but pity you
wouldn't get.

"When I was doing *Camille,* she knew how frightened I
was playing opposite Greta Garbo. But what could she
do? As an actress she respected another great actress and
Barbara knew I had to be on my toes. All she could do
was be there and try to get my mind off my fear. After all,
she was fighting Hollywood every day. I had MGM and
thank God I did."

Seldom did Barbara Stanwyck want a role desperately.
But in 1936 she told Joel McCrea, "I would give up
everything I own to make *Stella Dallas.*"

McCrea passed this on to Sam Goldwyn, but Goldwyn
said he wanted to test other actresses for the part. King
Vidor, who was to direct the film, said he wanted Stanwyck from the beginning, but Goldwyn would not relent.
He did not think she was the type to play Stella or that
she could carry it off effectively. He also thought she was
too young. But with McCrea and Vidor putting pressure
on Goldwyn he finally agreed to "allow" her to make a
screen test.

Barbara hit the roof! She was an established actress
with numerous prestigious credits. Besides, her memories
of screen tests terrified her: had she ever done a good one
other than the scene from *The Noose?* But Goldwyn
would not consider her for the part of Stella unless she
made a test like all the other actresses.

"The truth is Goldwyn didn't want me, period," she
said. "He was frank, I must admit. I wasn't capable of
doing it, he said. I was also too young. And I hadn't had
enough experience with children. When he finally agreed
to give me a test, Anne Shirley and I did the birthday
scene and it took a whole day. When Goldwyn saw it, he
gave me the part.

"The role was a challenging one for me because in the
first version Belle Bennett portrayed Stella. It was a double challenge actually, because Stella was two separate

women. On the surface she was loud and flamboyant with a touch of vulgarity, but beneath the surface she was fine, heartwarming and noble. Part of her tragedy was that while she recognized her own shortcomings, she was unable to live up to the standards she so painstakingly set for herself."

The story of Stella Dallas was a study of a mother's love and sacrifice. Her ambitions for her daughter, Laurel, were great and yet unselfish—so much so that Stella has to cut herself out of her child's life completely because she, as the mother, would be a drawback.

Stella did not have taste. She wore cheap gaudy clothes and had bad manners. It took her awhile to realize that people were staring at her because they were embarrassed. The realization that she would not fit into her daughter's life forced Stella into making a devastating decision: she would deliberately plan an affront that would free her daughter of any obligations.

It is ironic that in 1937 Stanwyck would play the sensitive role of a mother willing to make any sacrifice for her child because Barbara was preparing to send her own adopted son away to school.

Dion Fay, six years old, had not lived up to Stanwyck's expectations. The little boy was far from cute or perfect. Covered with freckles and overweight, Dion wore glasses and seemed to have little if any personality. And for whatever reason, mother and adopted son just never hit it off the way a mother and son should.

Sam Goldwyn asked Stanwyck before giving her the part of Stella: "How can you *feel* this part? *Have you ever suffered over a child?*"

Barbara said she had not. "But I can imagine how it would be," she sighed.

Her imagination went beyond expectations. Barbara as mother came off as if, indeed, she knew what suffering over a child was.

"Not only was Stella two people, so was Barbara," a

veteran Hollywood producer commented. "She was one personality on the movie set and another off the set. *Stella Dallas* was a prime example. If she had put one-tenth of the energy and devotion into bringing up her son that she put into the character of Stella, I could have admired her beyond the studio gates."

The *New York Times* review was like all the others: "Miss Stanwyck's portrayal is as courageous as it is fine. Ignoring the flattery of makeup and camera, she plays Stella as Mrs. Prouty drew her: coarse, cheap, common, given to sleazy dresses, to undulations in her walk, to fatty degeneration of the profile. And yet magnificent as a mother."

Barbara was elated. This picture was her finest work, deserving of an Oscar. Flying high, she was let down finding out Taylor was leaving for England to make *A Yank at Oxford*, the first Hollywood movie to be filmed in Europe.

"This is my only hope," he said, "If I don't come out of *Yank* with the right image, it won't be my fault or MGM's. I'd like to make it a good one, too, because this is a test for more movies to be made in Europe."

His trip was well publicized. Mobs of women were waiting for him everywhere. His cigarette butts were precious souvenirs and sold for high prices. Girls were hiding underneath his berth onboard the *Berengaria* thanks to the MGM publicity department. In England he was given a royal welcome, the first actor to make an American movie abroad.

As the rugged, cocky athlete in *A Yank at Oxford*, he exposed his hairy chest to the world and the world went wild. He played the role well, as if it were made for him, but the enormous publicity was difficult for him to accept since it was based on his masculinity and the "great exposure."

Meanwhile, Barbara was busy with *Breakfast for Two*

with Herbert Marshall. She was also thrilled over the new ranch Bob was building next to hers in Northridge. She was supervising the furnishings and completion of the house according to his wishes. The two houses—his and hers—stood on adjoining knolls.

But six months is a long time. Barbara knew he was young and had not been around. Girls were throwing themselves at him. His costars in *Yank* were Maureen O'Sullivan and Vivien Leigh. He knew little about women and their clever ways. Hadn't he been on the rebound from Irene Hervey and leaned on the first female shoulder strong enough to keep him going? Would he find this new freedom in England a refreshing relief from Hollywood, MGM—and her? All good reasons for Barbara to be concerned.

Cables went back and forth and telephone bills mounted as Barbara and Bob continued their romance miles apart. There were days when he felt terribly lonely. "And on one of those hopeless dreary days," he said, "I asked Barbara to marry me over transatlantic telephone."

She was reluctant. Not only was it a test of his virile image, it was also a test to see if they would feel the same way when he returned home. He had never been away from Hollywood, and he was just beginning to feel the sting of the press. There were so many lessons to be learned and before talking about marriage, he must concentrate on making *A Yank at Oxford:* as a turning point in his career, it could be the film that finally relieved him of the stigma he was suffering under the pretty boy image.

He wanted her to join him in England, but she was too busy with several film offers. Besides, Barbara was terrified of traveling and the very thought of a six-thousand-mile trip made her ill. She was content to remain in Hollywood, thank you, and needed no vacation. She wanted him to be alone. He had to see it through by himself and without her help. The press wanted to know if she was joining Taylor. "No," she replied, "I am not going to England to see Bob. He told me yesterday that the weather was not good and the filming was being delayed because of rain and he might not be home for Christmas."

"What about marriage?" they asked.

"We have no such plans," she replied. "and I have no intention of visiting Bob in Europe. Can you imagine what would happen if I went? It's bad enough here alone with you reporters. We wouldn't have a moment's peace!"

She went on to say that if the rain continued, their six-month separation would be extended. "Our transatlantic conversations will have to do for now. Guess you think it's silly talking about the weather, but at the moment our seeing each other depends on it."

He began calling her every day. As the production schedule of *A Yank at Oxford* continued to drag on, he pleaded with her to marry him. Barbara said her career came first and Bob hung up in a huff.

"Bob is still growing up," she confided to a friend in motherly fashion, "and I don't think he should be tied down. I want him to experience fame and fortune so he'll know what to do with both. Then he will have a better sense of values and will be capable of judging what is best for him."

It is doubtful that MGM would have allowed Taylor to go through with the marriage at that time anyway, and although Barbara's remarks about Bob's being too inexperienced with life made sense, she was wise enough to know that MGM would change his mind.

She was more career-minded than Taylor and knew what marriage would do to his image. Like Irene Hervey, she realized the importance of Bob's remaining single, but, unlike Irene, Barbara was willing to wait. She had to make Bob think it was she who was not ready and take the blame instead of MGM.

In December 1937 Taylor arrived home laden with

gifts for her and Dion. He made one more attempt to convince Barbara they should get married and once again she insisted they wait. But she agreed to a secret engagement.

She explained that Frank Fay had obtained a court order to compel her to let him see their son, Dion, and that Taylor had been mentioned as a consort. "It will be messy," she confided, "but I'll fight him all the way."

The court battle raged for weeks. On December 27, 1937, Barbara went on the stand to deny Frank's allegations that she would not allow him to see their adopted son for sixteen months "so that the child would become accustomed only to Robert Taylor."

Barbara said Fay was not in his right mind, that he struck her on more than one occasion, and on a drunken spree he threw Dion into the swimming pool.

Fay's attorney asked her: "Isn't the reason you are barring Mr. Fay from visiting the child because you want the boy to become accustomed to someone else—say Robert Taylor, for instance?"

Stiffening in the witness chair, Barbara answered, "No."

"Wasn't it a fact that you were having Mr. Taylor to your house frequently so that the child could forget Mr. Fay?"

"Mr. Taylor was at the house frequently, but it was not so the boy would forget his father."

"Did not Mr. Taylor give the boy gifts on numerous occasions?"

Barbara said that was true.

She was then asked about a check for fifty dollars that had apparently been made out to the child and signed by Taylor. The judge made the attorney withdraw the question. "I don't care how many times Mr. Taylor came to her house. This is her personal life and has nothing to do with this proceeding."

On January 16, 1938, Barbara went back on the stand

and said she demanded psychiatric examination of Frank Fay. She portrayed him as a man who mingled prayers with profanity, and she submitted ten affidavits in her attempt to show Fay to be of "unsound mind."

She described his peculiar habits. "When he passed a church, Frank would remove his hands from the wheel of a car and pray, endangering the lives of others." He got into a fist fight with the late Ted Healy, but had to stop to search for his false teeth when Healy knocked them out. Once at the Trocadero, she continued, Fay accused her of drinking too much champagne and knocked her down.

"He's an unfit guardian for the child," she said. "He drinks too much. He fell into Dion's crib once and fell asleep keeping the boy awake with his snoring. As far as I'm concerned he loves his new store teeth more than his son!"

She was asked if it was true that she owned fifty race horses and Barbara gave an affirmative answer.

"Is it true you spent most of Christmas Day at the races instead of at home with your child?" Fay's attorney asked.

She lowered her head and nodded.

Two days later the front page headlines of every newspaper blared the outcome: TAYLOR CITED. FIGHT IS LOST BY STANWYCK. The typical news story ran: "Robert Taylor's name was dragged into the Frank Fay–Barbara Stanwyck custody fight today when attorneys for Fay attempted to cast the number one heart throb of the screen in the role of a villian in the Santa Claus suit."

The judge ruled in favor of Fay. He would be allowed to visit his son twice a week and on alternating Saturdays, provided he was completely sober and always in the company of the child's nurse, who was obligated to report his conduct to Stanwyck.

Barbara commented as she was leaving court that her ex-husband was an all-time drunk. She told her lawyers to appeal.

As for Fay, he gave up the bottle eventually and became a hit as Elwood P. Dowd in the smash Broadway hit *Harvey.* He said, "How could I help getting along with a rabbit when I was named after Saint Francis of Assisi, who was the brother of all the birds and beasts."

On a coffee binge the rest of his life, Fay said he would talk about anything except one thing—his marriages!

The bitter court battle for custody rights to Dion was apparently only a revengeful tug-of-war between Barbara and Frank without real concern for the boy. She wanted Fay out of her life completely and Fay was not going to allow her to get away with anything. A mutual friend said, "If she wanted a broken cup worth a penny and he had thrown it in the garbage, she'd fight him and vice versa. Frank was not much better than Barbara as far as their son was concerned. He took advantage of his visitation rights and got bored soon after. That was that."

Barbara told reporters, "Above everything, I want my son to be happy. He needs a sense of security in the home, something I did not have as a child. I can't let him be thrown about like a piece of meat. He needs confidence and courage and love. But I don't want him to be one of the spoiled movie children. So I am sending him to a military school in the near future."

Dion was only six years old at the time. She had told the world that above everything she wanted her son to be secure and loved. Although she was at the race track on Christmas Day of 1937, a tender article appeared in a movie magazine about the special cozy Christmas she was planning for her little boy. The tree and the presents and the decorations, all to make him feel that he belonged. No one—not even his father—was going to harm this boy. No one would throw the child around like an abused mutt. She would protect him like a mother should, tuck him in at night, hold him close, and be there when he cried in his sleep.

It was a heartwarming article that undoubtedly convinced more moviegoers to see *Stella Dallas*, but Dion had no idea what it was to be held by his mother, or kissed by her. He doesn't remember her touching him unless there were photographers nearby. He cried, but no one came unless it was nanny.

Dion was sent to a military school six miles from Barbara's ranch. He was not invited home for the weekends or holidays nor did Barbara visit him. In the summertime he was sent to a camp on Catalina Island.

Slowly Barbara Stanwyck was shutting her son out of her life and in time reporters stopped asking about him. Out of sight, out of mind. Dion Fay eventually disappeared from all articles written about Stanwyck.

She did manage to see her son a total of ten days out of the year in the beginning, but that soon dwindled into nothing. Barbara was able now to begin a new life without the name Fay to interfere. She could concentrate on her career and on the man she would always love: Robert Taylor. She had never been happier professionally or romantically.

Nominated for an academy award for best actress for *Stella Dallas,* Stanwyck was sure she would win. On March 10, 1938, she and Bob attended the ceremonies at the Biltmore Hotel. This was Barbara's evening. Who would have thought that scrawny Ruby Stevens from Brooklyn, the kid with the dirty mouth and no real home, would be sitting in an expensive gown wearing gorgeous jewelry and fawned over by Hollywood society with an escort like Robert Taylor, the crown prince of Hollywood?

But as the awards for supporting players were given out, she was stunned that Anne Shirley, who had played her daughter, lost to Alice Brady for *In Old Chicago.*

No one really expected her to win. *Stella Dallas* was Shirley's first movie and, though her performance deserved the nomination, she lacked the Hollywood support veterans have.

Barbara had some tough competition—Luise Rainer for *The Good Earth*, Greta Garbo for *Camille*, Janet Gaynor for *A Star Is Born*, and Irene Dunne for *The Awful Truth*.

Luise Rainer had won the previous year for *The Great Ziegfeld* and had not bothered to attend this year. Greta Garbo was wonderful in *Camille*, but spoke much too softly. Irene Dunne was delightfully funny in *The Awful Truth*, but comedy performances weren't heavy contenders. Janet Gaynor was good, but lacked that certain something in *A Star Is Born*, and had already won the Award a few years back.

"And the winner is—Luise Rainer in *The Good Earth!*"

Barbara was shocked, incredulous, and disappointed. "My life's blood was in that picture," she said. "I should have won."

She never got over it and, though nominated again and again without winning, she regretted most the loss for *Stella Dallas*.

She had little to say about her follow-up, *Breakfast for Two*. "I had run the gamut with Stella," she explained, "and would not follow with another emotional role. So I gave the boys a chance. *Breakfast for Two* was Herbert Marshall's movie. I was playing, not working. I feel more comfortable in drama. It's my field, but comedy is relaxing. It's awfully easy, for me anyway—like a vacation."

Under nonexclusive contracts to both Twentieth Century–Fox and RKO, Barbara was sent many scripts but turned them all down. She had not won an Oscar, but her nomination meant she was worthy of winning it. Both studios had put her on suspension in late 1937 for not working. She turned to the Lux Radio Theater during this "vacation." When asked about being suspended, Stanwyck responded, "If you feel strongly enough, you must have the courage of your convictions to carry it through. That's my philosophy and it's gotten me into plenty of hot water. Somebody told me the other day that Bette Davis and I were the most suspended people in pictures, and wanted to know why we argued so much. I don't know about Bette, but the reason I argue is because I know myself. There are things I know I can do and other things I can't do.

"A lot of times a studio knows better than a star whether or not a picture will be a success. But I have to go on my instincts. Sometimes I've been wrong, but more often I've been right. Last year I was suspended for seven months because I wouldn't do two pictures at two different studios. They were rabid about these 'great' pictures. But neither one has yet to be made. That's vindication right there I think.

"I have to keep working to remain happy. They could work me every day and I'd love it. Those seven months away from the studio I didn't know what to do with myself. But if the same argument came up tomorrow, I'd probably go on another suspension. That's how I am."

Stanwyck spent most of her time on her ranch. Taylor was always running over to her swimming pool for a dip or she would stroll over to see him. They rode horseback at all hours, though at the time she was not especially keen on riding.

Taylor's three years before the camera as well as his bad experiences with the press sent him deeper into a quest for privacy. His life with Barbara made him withdraw even more. MGM no longer felt he needed to be seen so much in public and gradually they allowed him time to be alone. He was more flexible about his leisure than Barbara, who had only her work and watching her horses run at the track. Bob loved acting, but enjoyed many outdoor hobbies, one of their many differences.

Barbara suffered a major disappointment when Warner Brothers refused to allow her to play *Jezebel*, a film she wanted to do as much as she had craved *Stella Dallas*. But Warners wanted Bette Davis, who would go on to win an Oscar for her performance.

Finally Stanwyck completed her contract with Twentieth Century–Fox in *Always Good-bye* with Herbert Marshall. The theme was mother love and sacrifice but the film compared badly with *Stella Dallas*. Reviews were mild.

She pacified RKO by making *The Mad Miss Manton* in the summer of 1938. This would be the first of three films she would do with Henry Fonda, who complemented her the most of all screen partners on the screen, but their initial meeting was strained. Fonda made it obvious that he hated the part he was playing. He ignored everyone, including Stanwyck, except when the cameras were rolling. By just being himself he came across well on the screen and the critics liked *The Mad Miss Manton*.

Fonda said, "My close friendship with Barbara got off to a bad start. Three years later in *The Lady Eve*, I was delighted to see her and had forgotten about the *Manton* movie. When I tried to be friendly, she shouted, 'You son of a bitch! You paid no attention to me!' referring to *The Mad Miss Manton*. After that we got along famously."

A veteran Hollywood producer commented, "Stanwyck was not one to be snubbed. On her list of no-no's was any actor or actress who brought their personal feelings on the set. Being ignored by Fonda was so deliberately obvious, and under the circumstances Stanwyck would have treated him the same way and never forgiven him. But she was attracted to Fonda and he to her. They could feel the electricity during the love scenes. Nothing happened, according to them, but they never denied the attraction. As for Stanwyck, she proved it just by speaking to Fonda after his rudeness."

Maybe Henry Fonda wasn't paying attention to Barbara Stanwyck in 1938, but Cecil B. De Mille was. He admired her work so much that he offered her the lead in his classic film *Union Pacific* with Preston Foster and Joel McCrea. Stanwyck, as Mollie Monahan, had no problem with an Irish accent since she was brought up with a brogue. The critics loved the high-spirited energy and quick tongue of the engineer's daughter, a role Barbara handled easily.

The premiere was almost as exciting and spectacular as the movie itself. De Mille and the cast of *Union Pacific* took a five-day trip on a special Union Pacific train from Los Angeles to Omaha, Nebraska. Celebrations were held in towns and cities along the way. In Omaha parades of Sioux Indians with grand marshalls and state officials filled the town with applause. Three theaters premiered *Union Pacific* at the same time.

Before attending the gala celebration in Nebraska, Stanwyck had already begun *Golden Boy* at Columbia. This Clifford Odets play had been one of Broadway's greatest hits with John Garfield and Frances Farmer.

Harry Cohn, the man heavily responsible for getting Stanwyck started in films, wanted Garfield for the movie version, but director Rouben Mamoulian asked Cohn to consider a twenty-one-year-old newcomer who had just made an impressive screen test at Paramount. His looks were sensitive enough for the violin and he had the body of a prize fighter. Cohn decided to go with the unknown, William Holden.

The role of Joe, torn between music and boxing, was a heavy one even for an experienced actor. Holden had only done a few bit parts and he was terribly nervous. There was tension on the set each day as Cohn looked on critically. Holden tried to show self-confidence which was sadly lacking, by arguing with director Mamoulian, who realized he had made a mistake by thinking an inexperienced actor could handle the difficult role. Holden knew he was in trouble but studied the violin and took boxing lessons when he finished work on the set. He was averaging seventeen hours a day and surviving on nervous energy. After two weeks he was ready to crack and Cohn was ready to sack him.

Barbara stepped in only when she realized Cohn meant what he said. "You haven't given him a chance," she argued. "He's everything you want, but you won't leave him alone. I'll work with him every chance we get."

Holden was so grateful that Stanwyck had stuck her neck out for him he couldn't let her down when she offered to remain on the set every night to go over their lines. She tried to teach him little subtle camera tricks. Taylor, who often picked up Barbara, tried to help Holden also. "Hey," he said, "I was just like you once."

Between Stanwyck's and Taylor's help, Holden was not fired from *Golden Boy*, but Mamoulian was determined to make it as difficult as possible. He worked each scene the same way: the first a run-through, the second for tightening, and the third for actual filming. In order to squeeze all he could from the cast, he did not roll the camera on the third try. This put everyone on edge, with Holden feeling most of the pressure.

The day Mamoulian tried it on Stanwyck she swung around and yelled, "You ask me as a professional to work for you? Then don't ever tell me the camera's rolling when it isn't!"

Stanwyck not only fought for Holden, she gave him the best scenes in the movie. He never forgot what she did. Every year on the anniversary of the film's starting date, April 1, Holden sent the Queen, as he and Taylor referred to her, several dozen roses.

Although *Golden Boy* was the beginning of William Holden's successful career, a more important event took place off the set. On May 14, 1939, Barbara Stanwyck married Robert Taylor.

Four

*I*n 1938 such fan magazines as *Photoplay, Modern Screen, Silver Screen,* and *Screenland* were thrilling for the public to read, and enormously popular. They were the link between the great movie stars and their fans. Interviews, however, were carefully edited and all the photos touched up and released only by permission of the studios. Compared to the scandel sheets of today, the fan magazines were innocent and filled with brave tales or sad love stories and tidbits of gossip. Although "inside stories," which were written by press agents or studio publicity people, were harmless, they were fascinating and very juicy to the fans. But in 1938 *Photoplay* magazine rocked the boat, shocking the world with a scandalous article, "Hollywood's Unmarried Husbands and Wives." It cited five couples, including Carole Lombard and Clark Gable as well as Barbara Stanwyck and Robert Taylor: "Their houses are on adjoining knolls. The occupants ride together and work together and play together on their time off. If they're asked to a party—they're always invited together just like man and wife—they spend a quiet evening together at either one or the other's place."

The article relates the tragic story of actress Jean Harlow who was planning to marry actor William Powell when she died suddenly. *Photoplay* used this example to admonish Hollywood's unmarried couples: "And that, it seems, would point a lesson to the unique coterie of Hollywood's unwed couples—Bob Taylor and Barbara Stanwyck, who could get married if they really wanted to, George Raft and Virginia Pine, Carole Lombard and Clark Gable and the other steady company couples who might swing it if they tried a little harder. You can't take your happiness with you.

"For nobody, not even Hollywood's miracle men, has ever improved on the good old-fashioned, satisfying institution of holy matrimony. And, until something better comes along, the best way to hunt happiness when you're in love in Hollywood or anywhere else—is with a preacher, a marriage license and a bagful of rice."

In February 1939 Barbara and Bob announced their formal engagement when he gave her a diamond and ruby bracelet. They put both ranches up for sale but otherwise did not discuss marriage.

MGM was concerned about Clark Gable's divorce. Above all, Louis B. Mayer wanted no blemish of scandal to crop up around the stars in *Gone With the Wind*. Vivien Leigh was having an affair with Laurence Olivier and both were in the process of divorces, but little was known about them in America since they were popular only on the English stage. MGM used their influence to get Gable's freedom to marry Carole Lombard on March 29, 1939.

MGM did not have to worry about Taylor's pretty boy image any longer. In *The Crowd Roars* and *Stand up and Fight* he had established himself as a rugged actor—the "queer" stigma now forgotten. MGM had spent millions of dollars to create Robert Taylor, make him a star and a man's man. They were not going to allow a damaging article in a fan magazine to ruin all that.

He had been dating Barbara Stanwyck for three years and that was long enough.

The cameras were rolling on Robert Taylor and Hedy Lamarr in *Lady of the Tropics* when Mayer stopped production for twenty-four hours. MGM had made arrangements for a wedding, and on May 13 Barbara and Bob eloped. They drove to the home of Mr. and Mrs. Thomas Whelan in San Diego. Joining them were Zeppo and Marion Marx; Ida Koverman, Mayer's secretary; Buck Mack, Barbara's godfather; and Dale Frantz, a friend. The wedding party had a buffet supper, and after midnight, to avoid being married on the unlucky thirteenth day, the ceremony began in a room filled with roses.

Barbara was dressed in a new blue silk dress and a hat borrowed from her hairdresser, Holly Barnes, whose marriage Barbara had been a witness for the day before. Buck Mack gave the bride away.

She was very calm and spoke distinctly.

Taylor, in a brown business suit, was visibly shaken and he mumbled.

Judge Philip Smith was so nervous he cleared his throat several times and by the end of the ceremony could hardly talk.

The bride's wedding ring, a slender gold band circled with rubies, matched the bracelet Bob had given her.

At two in the afternoon the Taylors met the press at a reception at the Victor Hugo Café in Beverly Hills. Joel McCrea was the first to telephone congratulations, and William Holden sent a telegram—GOSH, WHAT A BLOW!—and signed it *Golden Boy.*

The Taylors said they had taken out their marriage license three days earlier under their real names, R. Stevens, age thirty-one, and Spangler Arlington Brugh, age twenty-seven. They admitted at the time they did not know exactly when or where the marriage would take place.

Taylor confessed years later that when MGM eventually gave in to his getting married, they masterminded the whole affair and he wasn't sure what was happening. "I wasn't even sure if I was in love. The only thing I was allowed to say about the whole thing was 'I do.'

"When I went to England, it was my first time away from everyone close to me and my career was on the line. I was lonely as hell. I think I wanted Barbara to come to England and marry me —just to relieve my panic and terrible loneliness.

"MGM never would have allowed it," he said. "And then I came home and everything turned out swell. I liked Barbara. She had done a lot of favors for me. There was no one else I admired more and no one else I cared to be with, but I kinda got over the urge to get married. When I knew it had to happen, I didn't know if I was in love . . . wasn't sure at all."

The *Daily News* wrote, "The Number One Heart Throb of the movies eloped with Barbara Stanwyck leaving the set of *Lady of the Tropics* and the beautiful Hedy Lamarr. There, there, girls, bear up and try not to take it too hard. You know it was ordained by fate."

The unwritten consensus of the press and the feeling of those who were close to the newlyweds was that it was Barbara Stanwyck who married Robert Taylor, not the other way around.

After the press reception, Barbara returned to her ranch, and Bob went to see his hysterical, sobbing mother, Ruth. She had called the doctor, who said if she continued to refuse food he might have to put her in the hospital, and he had to sedate her. When Bob walked in the door, she covered her face with her hands and wept. They talked—finally—and the word "wedding" was not mentioned: they referred to the marriage as "it."

Bob knew his mother would be depressed and ill. He

assured her nothing would change and tried to joke about it. "Oh, mother, you know when I'm working sometimes I get so tired I don't feel like driving all the way out to the ranch. I'll stay here often."

They had coffee, but Ruth complained that she felt sick and weak. "Will you check my heartbeat every so often during the night, just to make sure?" she asked.

Robert Taylor spent his wedding night with his mother.

Ruth had been ill with a weak heart when she was sixteen and doctors did not expect her to live through the birth of her only child. Taylor had taken care of her since he was a boy and could not desert her now. She would, ironically, outlive him.

The following morning he was back on the set with Hedy Lamarr going through another wedding in *Lady of the Tropics,* and Barbara returned to William Holden in *Golden Boy.*

At the time, both Stanwyck and Taylor were looking forward to booming careers. After a brief honeymoon in Bucks County, Pennsylvania, at the home of playwright Moss Hart, they returned to their hectic schedule.

Barbara's next picture, Paramount's *Remember the Night* with Fred MacMurray, was one of her best. The *New York Times* noted with enthusiasm, "Perhaps this is a bit too early in the season to be talking of the best movie of 1940. It is not too early to say that Paramount's nomination is worth considering."

Another remarkable trait of Stanwyck's was revealed during the production of *Remember the Night,* after she had already been dismissed for the day and it was discovered she was scheduled to do another scene. Frantically the assistant director ran to her dressing room. To his amazement she was still in costume and makeup. "I never leave until everyone else does," she remarked, "just in case."

Taylor's assignment in *Flight Command* was the beginning of the end of his marriage. He became so involved with his role as a navy ensign that he decided to take flying lessons and spent every minute of his spare time in the air with his instructor. On top of this, he was spending too much time fishing with Spencer Tracy or at the Hunt Club with Clark Gable—or so Barbara felt. She was terrified of airplanes and afraid of guns. When Taylor polished his rifles, she often ordered him out of the house. "Everytime you aim that thing you scare me to death," she said.

At least hunting and fishing kept him on the ground. His passion for airplanes upset Barbara very much. "Bob's not satisfied on the ground anymore," she complained, but no matter how much he pleaded with her to fly with him, she cringed at the thought. She was patient with him, giving into his hobbies and pleased that he was not completely wrapped up in acting, but she felt they were not spending enough time together. Despite the fact their ranches had not been sold, Barbara began scouting for a house in town. Through it all Stanwyck was a city girl. She even disliked traveling by car for any distance.

She found a furnished home in Bel-Air. The occupants were willing to rent and Barbara decided immediately it was best for her and Bob to grab this opportunity. He did not agree, and he tried to talk Barbara out of moving.

"I don't want to live in a furnished house," he said.

"But it's only temporary," she insisted.

"Why can't we wait until we sell the ranches? What's the big rush?"

"We're both so busy," she said. "My days off are not always your days off, and when they do coincide we don't see each other. Commuting takes too much time."

"How can I leave my gun rack?"

She shook her head.

"And my kitchen was designed to my liking," he said. "What about all my gadgets?"

"All we need is a can opener."

"I can't live that way. I'm not used to living in someone else's house without my own things."

"Just keep saying to yourself it's only temporary."

"And the horses?" he squawked. "We can't just leave them."

"They are in good hands."

"But I can't ride when I feel like it."

"You always have your airplane!"

The Taylors moved to Los Angeles and Bob felt fenced in. He loved the country and considered Northridge his first real home. He raised quarter horses and was as close to each one as he had been to his own horse, Gypsy, back in Nebraska. Barbara's thoroughbreds were for the sport of winning at the track. She had no favorites.

Confinement in Los Angeles sent Taylor soaring in his plane more frequently. "I was free up there, nobody telling me what to do or how to do it. No telephones or obligations. Free as hell."

Barbara rarely had free time. Completely dedicated to her career, she was either busy reading potential scripts or making a movie and learning her lines. When she was free, she preferred reading a good book and relaxing at home. MGM told Taylor what his next movie would be, who his costars were, and how they wanted him to perform. He was always on time and knew his lines, but the preparation and productions were entirely different than for Barbara, who felt completely responsible to herself and no one else. When he left the movie set, he left his character at the studio. Barbara did not. When she was making a movie, she was on cue all the time and completely consumed by the project. If they had anything in common as a married couple, it was their disinterest in socializing or entertaining. She had never felt comfortable with Hollywood society after the bitterness of her life in California as Mrs. Frank Fay. Taylor had been forced by MGM to be seen at the right places with the right people

as a young newcomer, but with few exceptions he no
longer had to face the mobs of women who tore his
clothes off. The problems arose when the Taylors had the
same day off. She wanted his company, but he was bored.
He wanted to get into his plane or go skeet shooting. Barbara preferred he hang around until she was rested
enough to chat with him or have the dinner he usually
prepared.

"Bob loves the kitchen," she said. "He collects cook-
books and all kinds of gadgets. I can't boil water. When
he's home, he is happy only in the kitchen. Otherwise he's
always looking out the window."

Taylor was busy making mediocre films in 1940. His
career was in a slump and his life at home just as dull.
Louis B. Mayer, referring to Bob's plane—and his
career—told the actor, "What goes up, must come down,
son. It's not easy being a star, and even the best of 'em
have slumps. Take your idol, Spencer Tracy. When he
couldn't get a job in this town, we put him under contract.
I thought he was finished and so did everyone else. He
had been arrested for drunkenness and resisting arrest in
Arizona. So, who needed Spence? He was a troublemaker
like Wallace Beery. But we all kept the faith and you
know the rest. If it can happen to Tracy, it can happen to
you. Besides, have I ever failed you, son?"

Taylor said, "No."

Barbara tried to help: "There's no explaining why one
gives a polished peformance in one picture and yet with a
good script is rotten in the next." She said Bob's problem
was that his career was never on an even keel—rather
very good or very bad. "Actors, if they are lucky," she explained, "go along doing well, and the critics say 'good
performance' about anything they do." Taylor was not
destined to follow this pattern.

He said his form of courage was survival, and Barbara
agreed. He was taking another beating, but he had
survived the initial attack in the pretty boy era of the con-

tinuous newspaper bombardments and the radio commentators' venom. Now he would have to survive the lemons that bore his name on the marquees.

"When I was about convinced I had been forgotten," he said, "MGM handed me the script of *Waterloo Bridge*. It was an actor's dream and the role fitted me like a pair of custom-made shoes." It would remain Taylor's favorite film during his long career.

Perhaps it was the opening scene—Taylor standing in a heavy fog on a bridge looking down over the Thames and reflecting on his dead love, his hair sprinkled with gray—that told the audiences this was the Taylor they had been waiting for, the actor he really was: Taylor, the passionate, loyal lover every woman ached for.

Since it was the custom of all English officers during World War I to wear a mustache, he was required to wear one—the mustache he was to shave off and grow again with monotonous regularity throughout his career. It did, however, give him the distinction and maturity that transformed a juvenile pretty face into one of character.

Waterloo Bridge was the second movie Taylor made with Vivien Leigh, who had won an Oscar for her performance in *Gone With the Wind*.

Taylor's popularity was restored not only with the younger generation but with their parents as well. He was back on top, but this time as a serious motion picture performer, not a freak.

While Taylor was filming *Waterloo Bridge* in England, Barbara was doing a series of excellent pictures back home. When her favorite director Frank Capra formed his own production company and called her about making *Meet John Doe* with Gary Cooper, she responded immediately with "Send the script right over, Frank!"

Capra said he didn't have a script. She wanted to know if her part was an honest one and he promised her it was. Stanwyck agreed to do *Meet John Doe* without first seeing the script, and Gary Cooper did, too, followed by Edward Arnold, Walter Brennan, and Spring Byington.

"There is no one like Frank Capra," she said. "He is in a class all by himself. It is a joy watching him work every day. You make other pictures to live, but you live to make a Capra picture."

Moviegoers could easily identify themselves with the naturalness of Stanwyck and Cooper, an ideal pair. Cooper, known to have affairs with his leading ladies, did not attempt one with Barbara. He was a nice guy with little personality who preferred society women, money, and power. He got all three but still maintained a dull and harmless simplicity perfect for the part of John Doe, a regular guy who wants to help mankind and make the world a better place. Barbara plays a hard-boiled reporter who eventually has her cynical views mellowed by the example of Cooper.

Because the story of *Meet John Doe* dealt with the threat of fascism, Capra filmed four different endings and the picture was released in various cities with contrasting endings. Capra decided on a fifth that was the final print.

Film Daily picked *Meet John Doe* as one of the ten best pictures of the year. The *New York World-Telegram*, believing that Stanwyck and Cooper were in top form, wrote enthusiastically, "They don't come any better than this one."

Stanwyck's good luck continued when Paulette Goddard and Charlie Chaplin got married, thanks to the *Photoplay* article, and the honeymooning bride had to turn down the female lead in *The Lady Eve* with Henry Fonda. Stanwyck was signed and reunited with "that son of a bitch who ignored me three years ago!"

The "mad genius," Preston Sturges, wrote the screenplay and directed the comedy hit. Stanwyck plays the role of Jean Harrington, gambler and flirt, who cleverly impersonates the sophisticated and witty Lady Eve Sidwich.

Stanwyck's wardrobe was high fashion, a first for her. Edith Head, the famous dress designer, was assigned to *The Lady Eve*. "Barbara hated high fashion," the designer recalled. "She cared less what she was wearing in a film as long as it wasn't form-fitting or tight around the waist. The gowns created for Eve were tight and slick. I knew Barbara could wear them very well because she had fine posture, a good figure and was delightfully slim. When I discussed her glamorous wardrobe, Barbara kept quiet. I knew she preferred loose-fitting garments, but the first dress she had to put on was a clinging black crepe with a very high and very tight cummerbund.

"She was suffering at first. And then I noticed another strange trait. She kept her back to the mirror and she would not turn around because she saw no need to! She said that people notice you sideways or from the back, but I just insisted that she face the mirror. When she did, Barbara was stunned. She didn't say it because of her modesty when it came to her attractiveness, but she was delighted. From then on Barbara wanted to wear high fashion. I understand this was one of the very few times she ever changed her mind about anything.

"We had only one dispute and she won. Most actresses model their costumes in front of the camera for the director, hands on hip and a flare here and there, turning around once or twice before walking away. Barbara, on the other hand, walked toward the camera, stood perfectly still, turned around and left the room! I told her to please put her hand on her hip and pose.

"Barbara looked at us expressionless and said firmly, 'I am not a model so why should I act like one!' And that was that. Barbara's clothes became a part of her, anyway, as soon as the cameras were rolling. I worked for her in twenty-three films and if she didn't like something, she said so. She was not one of those actresses who praises a dress and then says it stinks behind my back."

The Lady Eve was chosen by the National Board of Review as one of the best pictures in 1941.

Stanwyck bloomed as a result of her newfound elegance and sophistication. Otherwise she would not have agreed to play the part of the beautiful woman in *The Great Man's Lady*. If any of her previous parts called for attractiveness, that was all right, but if the description called for "a beauty," Stanwyck shied away. She remembered what Capra told her in the beginning of her career. "You're trying to be beautiful," he had said and emphasized that she was what she was and not to pretend she was anything more. But with elegant gowns created by Edith Head and expensive jewelry to complement the wardrobe, Stanwyck was convincing as a stunning aging woman in *The Great Man's Lady* with Joel McCrea.

She gave an Oscar-quality performance in this movie, but was nominated instead for *Ball of Fire* opposite Gary Cooper. At the awards ceremony, Stanwyck was not as excited or as confident as she had been at the one for *Stella Dallas*. As usual, her competition was severe: Greer Garson for *Blossoms in the Dust,* Olivia de Havilland for *Hold Back the Dawn,* Joan Fontaine for *Suspicion,* and Bette Davis for *The Little Foxes.*

Joan Fontaine went home with the Oscar in 1941.

Taylor was also doing well for himself. His portrayal of *Billy the Kid* was excellent—and in color. With Joan Crawford and Greer Garson in *When Ladies Meet* he held his own in light comedy. But it was his role of a racketeer in *Johnny Eager* that was acclaimed. It had meaning to him, too, because he fell helplessly in love with his costar Lana Turner. Only twenty-one years old, Turner already held the title of Sweater Girl and was suing Artie Shaw for divorce after less than a year of marriage.

Taylor told a friend that both he and Lana were

"bursting" with passion during the filming of *Johnny Eager*, but did not get together until they finished the movie—at least, that was what he claimed. Casually he said, "I had to have her if only for one night!" Lana claims their passion was never consummated.

Apparently there was more to it than that. Taylor admitted not being happy with Barbara and said he would ask for a divorce. Lana panicked. "Don't do anything drastic," she pleaded. "And, above all, don't tell Barbara!"

Lana made it clear that she did not want to be the solution to his bad marriage. But Taylor, whether terribly innocent or absolutely sure what he was doing, braced Barbara for divorce and told her he was in love with Lana Turner, who was fourteen years younger than Stanwyck.

Turner admits to a mutual attraction and that she flirted with him. Their love scenes in *Johnny Eager* were some of the hottest and most convincing in years. According to producer Norman Lear, the sexiest woman in the world was "Lana Turner, as she was held in the arms of Robert Taylor in the terrace scene in *Johnny Eager*."

Although Turner was extremely young, her love life had been rocky, especially the affair with attorney Greg Bautzer, her first lover. Joan Crawford wasn't ashamed to admit her love for Bautzer, and she was determined to have him to herself. When she could take no more of his "silly affairs," Crawford invited Lana to her house "for a little chat."

Crawford announced Bautzer's love for her. It had been mutual for a long time so there was no reason for Lana to build up her hopes. Greg was too much of a gentleman— or cad—to tell the truth, though he undoubtedly would have enjoyed carrying on his dual life had it not been for Crawford. Naturally Lana was humiliated and hurt. According to Joan, it was for the best since Lana was young and vulnerable.

When Joan Crawford's friend, Barbara Stanwyck, indirectly entered Lana's life, an open relationship with

Taylor would have been too much of a burden. He was everything Lana wanted, but the price was too high.

Taylor told a reporter that his newest costar, Lana Turner, was perfectly proportioned and not as "busty" as her pinup photos. "Her face is delicate and beautiful," he said. "I have never seen lips like hers and though I was never known to run after blondes, Lana could be the exception. I couldn't take my eyes off her. Her voice was like a breathless little girl. I don't think she knew how to talk without being sexy. When she said a simple thing like 'good morning,' I melted. She is the type of girl a guy would risk five years in jail for rape."

After his confession to Barbara he went to Lana, but she turned him down. She was attracted to him, yes, but not in love with him, and the last thing she wanted was to break up his marriage. Taylor proposed to her. It would not be an affair. He was seriously in love. Lana shied away. Bob went home to Barbara, who moved out for a few days. She stayed at the home of her faithful maid, Harriet Coray, but could not stay away from Taylor.

Gossip had been spreading about the Taylors' strained marriage earlier in the year because they were separated most of the time. Barbara met with the press in Hollywood saying, "Bob is tired. He has made several pictures in a row with no time off in between—and he's resting now.

"He wanted to take some extensive flying lessons and took his instructor to the Odlum Ranch in Palm Springs. We are by no means separated and there are people, I suppose, who are jealous and would like to see me take a fall. Since my career has been successful lately, they attacked my marriage."

When asked if she were going to have a baby, Barbara looked the reporter straight in the face and said she would shout it to the world if that were the case.

"Bob and I are building a house in Beverly Hills," she

said, changing the subject. "Does that sound as if we're getting a divorce? The new house will be small and cozy with a living room, small den, dining room, and kitchen downstairs; upstairs there will be four bedrooms—one for Bob and me, one for Dion, one for Buck Mack [Barbara's godfather]—and a servant's room."

Still the rumors persisted. The Taylors were never seen at parties or dining out or driving together in the family car or sitting in their backyard or walking together in or out of the house.

Bob sent a letter, dated March 14, 1941, to Jim Reid of *Motion Picture* magazine.

> Dear Jim:
> Thank you for the opportunity of replying to the rumor which seems to have been circulating around recently. Unfortunately, it is an opportunity which is too seldom granted people in this business.
> Barbara and I were married two years ago for reasons which are common, I believe, to any two people who decide to take that step, namely love, mutual interests and a pretty good understanding of each other. So far as we are concerned these elements still exist.
> The rumor, though unfortunate, did not come as a surprise to either Barbara or myself. Actually we have been expecting it. It seems most inevitable that when picture people have been married over a year, rumors of this sort arise. May I assure you and hope that you will assure your readers in turn, that all such rumors are entirely unfounded and untrue. Thanks again for Barbara and myself.
>
> > Sincerely,
> > Bob

Maybe the public was satisfied with the Taylors' statements, but their close friends saw a strained marriage even before the Lana Turner incident. Barbara continued her maternalistic instincts, affectionately referring to Bob

as Junior, and he still called her the Queen. One acquaint-
ance quipped: "Maybe they forgot each other's names,
they're apart so often." Paradoxically, though, those sepa-
rations held the marriage together as long as it did. If they
had been forced to live under the same roof seven days a
week, neither could have tolerated the other for very long.

Since Barbara was not a traveler, the majority of her
movies were made in Hollywood. If she had to get anywhere, it was always by train. On the very few trips she
and Bob made together, he would fly and she would find
other means of transportation to meet him at their destination. She liked to be close to her work and never took
vacations, concentrating all her efforts on her career.

Bob, who early in his film career had enjoyed going
back to his hometown, Beatrice, Nebraska, stayed away
after his marriage. He was aware that she would not fit in.
She had always been a city girl and was bored with country living. Small-town folks had little in common with her
and vice versa. Barbara might insult someone without
realizing it. Her outlook was straightforward, and she let
it be known, and her vocabulary—filled with expletives—
would also be a problem in a small Midwestern town.

Taylor's classic understatement to the press, "Miss
Stanwyck is not the sort of woman I would have met in
Nebraska," was certainly one of the truest things he ever
said.

And there was his mother Ruth, a domineering influence in his life, but he knew how to handle her. She had
always been a frail woman and he gave in more than he
should have. Inevitably there was no love between Ruth
and Barbara—both wanting all his attention and both
wanting to be the boss. He had two mothers: one he could
visit once a week, the other shared his bed.

Taylor had been brought up a gentle and sensitive
young man. His idea of the perfect woman was one who
was a lady, spoke softly, was a good cook, wanted to have

children, was not in show business, wore frilly feminine clothes in soft colors, and let him be the boss, right or wrong.

He married the wrong woman, but what troubled him most was his deep devotion and respect for Barbara. "Besides," he said years later, "it's tough hurting someone you know loves you sincerely and would do anything for you."

Barbara did not mind Bob's making movies away from home. She did not interfere with his career. Although she complained about his hunting, she bought him several expensive rifles to show that she was sorry for complaining about his hobbies.

Their press agent, Helen Ferguson, said: "It's true Barbara treated Bob like a little boy because that was how she saw him. It was he who said he was just a kid from Nebraska. Barbara did not want to see him get hurt as she had been. She was too protective. And she meant well telling him what to do and how to do it. This was her way of helping. Bob wanted to be the man of the house, and Barbara did not know how to accept that, despite the fact she insisted he was. Bob was like most men. He did not want to be alone nor did he want to live with Ruth. He was a sticker and that's why he tried to make the marriage work."

Lana Turner claims that to this day Stanwyck will not speak to her. Turner made an attempt not long ago and was deliberately and definitely snubbed for something that happened over forty years ago. She would not be the only one.

The Turner–Taylor incident was covered up. No one knew about Barbara's moving out or the reconciliation. But in October 1941 Barbara was rushed to Cedars of Lebanon Hospital with severed arteries on her wrist and arm. She was treated and released the same day. Those in the know in Hollywood speculated that she had attempted suicide. She laughed it off by saying she had tried to open a permanently closed window in their Beverly Hills home and accidentally broke the glass and injured her arm. When the press hounded her about the "unfortunate accident," indicating there must be more to it, Stanwyck refused to discuss the matter.

Her exceptionally deep love for Taylor, however, was an emotion she could not control. He was everything to her—son, lover, husband, companion, and cook. Although she knew her way around and had the ability to handle most situations, Barbara knew she could not control love and fidelity. Neither success nor money could either. If Bob had strayed only two years after marriage, clearly he was not satisfied at home. It is doubtful Barbara would look the other way if he began a series of one-night stands, but his claiming to be in love with Lana and wanting to marry her was an especially deep hurt for Barbara to overcome. Who would replace Lana?

Taylor was scheduled to make *Her Cardboard Lover.* His costar, Norma Shearer, was not his type. But *Stand by for Action* and *Bataan* were war movies with all male casts, thank God.

Barbara, however, faced another problem at the beginning of the United States entry into World War II. Bob desperately wanted to get into action. Why, she pleaded with him, would anyone want to volunteer to get killed? At thirty-one, he was too old for combat, but Taylor was working every angle to get to the front. MGM held him back for *Song of Russia.* Not only did he hate the movie, but being left behind put him in a depressed and restless mood. Clark Gable, Jimmy Stewart, and Tyrone Power were already in various branches of the service.

Barbara tried to understand his eagerness, but how was that possible if she had no tolerance for hunting rifles, fishing tackle, and skeet shooting? Wasn't it bad enough he could get hurt at the Hunt Club or flying that dangerous airplane? Now he wanted to rush into a war when he really didn't have to. He could sell war bonds or make patriotic films. Taylor would not listen to such maternal rubbish. He volunteered and was sworn into the United States Navy in February 1943—under the name of Spangler Arlington Brugh, even though he and Barbara had legally adopted their stage names a few days before.

He applied for active duty but was turned down. Instead he was assigned to the navy's Aviation Volunteer Transport Division as lieutenant, junior grade—the customary rank given to men over thirty who have a civilian pilot's license. Taylor had 110 flying hours to his credit. He took his basic training at the naval air station in Dallas, Texas, then was transferred to the naval instructors' school in New Orleans as a student. When he graduated, he requested active duty but was turned down again. He remained in New Orleans as a flying instructor.

Another instructor, Tom Purvis, became a close lifetime friend. "Taylor was nervous in the beginning," Purvis said, "because he figured I had him pegged as a handsome Hollywood star and nothing else. The first time we went up together he did a right slow roll and it was perfect but, when we came out of it, Taylor looked like he was going to throw up. I asked him what was wrong."

"Hell, I just lost my cigarette lighter," he cried. "It's down there in the Mississippi River!"

"So what?" I laughed.

"So what!" Taylor yelled. "That was a solid gold Zippo with a raised gold replica of the naval station emblem. Barbara gave it to me. She'll flip her lid! What the hell do I tell her? A three-hundred-dollar lighter is at the bottom of the Mississippi River?"

"Yeh," Tom said. "Tell her just that. If you ask me, it's funny!"

"You don't know Barbara," was Taylor's reply.

She replaced it, however, on her only visit to New Orleans while Taylor was stationed there. He arranged a party for her at the elegant Roosevelt Hotel.

Purvis said, "I can understand how Taylor felt about that lighter, but he wasn't just annoyed. The guy was scared just like a kid who lost an expensive toy and was terrified to go home and tell Mommy. That incident told me more than Taylor ever did."

There was no publicity about her visit to Taylor. He wouldn't allow it. He was all navy now and cared little about what was happening in Hollywood. On one of his furloughs to California he agreed to pose with Barbara in their home. He looked very young with his butch cut and Barbara very mature and sophisticated in her dressing gown with upswept hair. The pictures released showed a much-posed Robert Taylor in uniform trying to look interested in the domestic scene.

He said he felt more comfortable in New Orleans and that he resented publicity when he was in navy dress. Bob told Purvis often that he had never been happier since his days in Nebraska. "It seems everything I do is corny," he said. "Mayer thinks it's cute that I'm quite content in the navy. So does Barbara. Sometimes I feel as though they are letting their little boy have his fun."

Except for missing Bob, Stanwyck at this time had never been more content with her career. Oddly she had become the highest-paid woman in the movies—outearning the other cinema queens of the day, Bette Davis, Greer Garson, and Betty Grable—but she was rarely listed in the popularity polls. Her press agent, Helen Ferguson, said that was because Barbara was not a sex symbol. She was getting the best scripts in Hollywood, and publicity about her marriage was better than ever.

When he was on furlough, Taylor told the press, "Just for luck I'm wearing a Saint Christopher's medal around my neck. Barbara's worried, so when she gave it to me, I put it on. If it does me any good, why not?"

Barbara was radiant hearing him say that. Reporters looked at one another when she said, "Bob looks so young with that short haircut and he's lost around ten pounds. He is the most handsome man I've ever seen, but he looks eighteen. People will think I'm his mother!"

One reporter said, "I'm very surprised she came out with that one."

Warner Brothers' *The Gay Sisters* with George Brent was a successful film for Stanwyck, but *Lady of Burlesque* for United Artists was beneath her at this stage of her career. Based on the novel *The G-String Murders* by Gypsy Rose Lee, *Lady of Burlesque* was an unfortunate reminder of Brooklyn-raised chorus girl Ruby Stevens. Included among the song and dance routines with high heels, cartwheels, and splits was her throaty rendition of "Take It Off the E-String, Play It on the G-String."

The *New York Times* gave Stanwyck a gentle slap in the face by writing "She hasn't forgotten her early chorus training on Broadway, but the *Brooklyn Daily Eagle* was milder with, "Barbara Stanwyck is a lively girl and knows her way around roles like this."

The consensus was was that Stanwyck should not have made the movie. She was not the type to hide her background, but now that she was a renown dramatic actress, why flaunt the fact she had been a hoofer? Why bother with a limp script, scanty costumes, and the bumps and grinds? Certainly it wasn't for the money. Nor was it for an Academy Award nomination.

Joan Crawford said she would have done it "for fun" because she had been a hoofer, too, but her need to impress Hollywood elite society was too strong for her to "descend" to such a role. Barbara, though, didn't give a hoot for Hollywood society.

Her next effort, the peculiar *Flesh and Fantasy* with Charles Boyer, was more suited to Stanwyck's status as classy actress. Three stories linked together with commentary, it dealt with fate versus free will. It was rated good, but not extraordinary.

Nothing mattered to Barbara when she got her hands on Billy Wilder's script for *Double Indemnity* and her teeth into the role of Phyllis Dietrichson.

She had one fear, however. "I had never played a cold-blooded killer before. Phyllis was calculating and hard. I wasn't sure I wanted to do anything like this despite the fact I adored the story."

Wilder told her that Fred MacMurray would do the movie if she would. "Give me a little time to think it over," she said.

Wilder talked to MacMurray, who felt the same way Barbara did. He had always played the easygoing nice guy and wasn't sure if moviegoers would accept him as a dirty louse. "And I'm not sure if I want to do it," he said.

Wilder mentioned casually that Barbara Stanwyck agreed to do *Double Indemnity* if MacMurray did. This was too big for MacMurray to turn down because he admired Stanwyck and knew she would not do the film unless she was sure of it. "Okay," he told Wilder. "I'll do it."

Wilder did not mention that his first choice, George Raft, had turned down the part. "Nobody wanted to play a murderer in those days except a guy like Raft," Wilder said.

The grim story of Phyllis Dietrichson persuading insurance investigator Walter Neff to fix her husband up with an accident policy and murder him so they can collect $100,000 on its double indemnity clause is a classic by now.

Stanwyck fans were shocked when she made her first appearance on screen in *Double Indemnity* wearing a blonde wig and ankle bracelet. Wilder said he wanted her to look as cheap and sleazy as possible.

Double Indemnity was nominated for best picture, best actress, cinematography (black and white), music (scoring of a dramatic or comedy picture), sound recording, and writing. This was Barbara's third nomination; this time she lost to Ingrid Bergman for *Gaslight.*

Stanwyck said, "I'm beginning to feel like one of Crosby's also-ran horses!" But she said playing the part of a "ruthless broad" who murders without blinking an eye had opened new dimensions for her. She was not limited now. Wilder warned her it would take guts and he knew if any actress had plenty of that, it was Barbara Stanwyck. But guts could not erase the disappointment losing the Oscar for the third time. Her total dedication blended with sterling talent in three entirely different roles, the heartbreaking *Stella Dallas,* the funny dancer in *Ball of Fire,* and now the murderess in *Double Indemnity,* demonstrated her awesome versatility.

She had gained the respect of every studio and director in Hollywood, and every one of her costars. Money was not a problem. She cared even less for grand compliments. She had power, but rarely used it. She had married one of the handsomest movie actors in the world, who just happened to be one of the nicest. But Barbara Stanwyck had yet to run up on stage to accept the highest award presented to an actress—the Oscar!

My Reputation, a love story with George Brent, was released for viewing by servicemen overseas before appearing in the United States. After a brief appearance in *Hollywood Canteen,* Barbara filmed a delightful picture with Dennis Morgan. In *Christmas in Connecticut* she portrays a columnist for *Smart Housekeeping* who's all phony because she (like the real Barbara Stanwyck) could not boil an egg. She is forced to entertain a young serviceman (Morgan) complete with fake baby and husband. The movie was fun to make and more fun to watch. It focused on a typical New England Christmas, including romantic sleigh rides, dancing the Virginia reel, lots of snow, and the antics of S. Z. Sakall. No critic dared say a bad word about *Christmas in Connecticut* for fear of being lynched.

In January 1945 Robert Taylor went to New York City on a war bond drive and to promote the navy film *The Fighting Lady*. Barbara joined him and made it clear to the press that her being in the East was to see her husband and not for professional reasons. But when Earl Wilson telephoned Barbara, she agreed to an interview. When Wilson arrived at the Taylors' hotel suite, he found himself alone with Bob, who said Barbara would be back shortly. When she finally did appear, she rushed into the room, said hello, and fled into the bedroom muttering something about needing a shower.

Meanwhile Wilson carried on a lengthy conversation with Taylor. Bob was impatient because he was bored with small talk, and Wilson was impatient because he expected an exclusive interview with Barbara Stanwyck. An hour passed. Taylor occasionally banged on the bedroom door but got no response. He was annoyed but spoke about the navy and his return to filmmaking when the war ended.

Taylor was trim and unusually handsome in his uniform, Wilson said, but mentioned casually that if Bob's fans were fickle, he could get out of acting and find something else to do. The navy had changed him, and Hollywood wasn't that important if he had to start all over again.

The strained "interview" continued and Taylor knocked on the locked bedroom door again and again. Wilson finally left, annoyed and disappointed. His column the following day was devoted to Lieutenant Taylor and how rude Barbara had been. "Did she need a shower *that* badly?"

Several nights later Barbara ran into Earl Wilson at a nightclub. She approached him graciously and gave her reasons for avoiding the interview. Barbara explained that she never should have agreed to it because Bob was on an official visit to promote *The Fighting Lady* and to sell war bonds. Being at his side was her wifely duty but she did not want to take attention away from him. Furthermore, it was up to her as a loyal American citizen during wartime to back Bob and not to overshadow him in any way. Wilson was so impressed by Barbara's humble explanation that he wrote a retraction applauding her.

Taylor was sent to Illinois to await his discharge papers, and Barbara returned to Humphrey Bogart playing a psychotic murderer in *The Two Mrs. Carrolls.*

On November 5, 1945, Taylor was discharged from the navy. Reporters asked him how it felt to be going home. "I'm not sure," he said. "I met some great guys and it's rough splitting up the group. I liked the navy. You know exactly who you are and what's expected of you."

Reporters asked him if he had considered making a career out of the navy. "I have given it serious thought," he replied. Reluctantly Taylor flew back to his wife and to a Hollywood filled with the competition presented by exciting new leading men like Cornel Wilde, Van Johnson, Frank Sinatra, and Peter Lawford.

Upon his return Taylor did not ask MGM for a raise because he would get killed by taxes. Instead the studio gave him a new twin-engine Beechcraft worth $75,000. Ralph Couser, one of his navy buddies, was hired by MGM and assigned as Taylor's copilot. Couser and Purvis became Bob's closest buddies.

Taylor's main concern was his comeback picture. He was thrilled with his costar, Katharine Hepburn, but *Undercurrent* was a disappointment. The critics, however, were unusually kind to him by welcoming him back to the screen and commenting on how relaxed he was after a three-year absence.

Clark Gable said, "Don't worry, baby, they did the same to me! Put me in *Adventure* with Greer Garson, a lovely lady but a rotten movie, and the headlines read: GABLE'S BACK AND GARSON'S GOT HIM. That's all I heard on every street corner." Gable hit the bottle heavily, drove too fast—resulting in one accident—and dated every socialite he met, searching for another Carole Lombard, who had died tragically in a plane crash on a war bond tour. Taylor and Gable became good friends.

Nothing was too fast for the two of them. If Barbara wanted Bob on the ground, he'd stay there—on a motorcycle with Clark cycling at top speed beside him. Keenan Wynn and Gary Cooper were usually not far behind.

Louis B. Mayer was furious. They were too reckless, he said, taking out their frustrations by tearing up the roads and anything else in their way.

Barbara was busy with Robert Cummings in *The Bride Wore Boots*. Ironically her name in the film was Missy, the same nickname her maid had given her. Over the years her costars began referring to her as Missy because Harriett was usually on the set and the name caught on. Not just anyone could use this endearing term. You had to be a close and loyal friend or coworker.

Cummings said Missy was a great person and one of his reasons came about the day he had done thirteen retakes as a steeplechase rider. Director Irving Pichel was ready to make him do a fourteenth—despite the heat, another change of horses, and a tired cast of riders, who mumbled and complained to one another. Then silence reigned as Barbara walked slowly across the grass from her trailer. She faced the director and said, "Mr. Pichel, if Bob Cummings rides that race once more, you will never direct me in another scene!" She stood for one stern moment, then turned and took another long slow walk back to her trailer. She won her point and the respect of everyone on the set of *The Bride Wore Boots*—an example of Stanwyck's power used well.

She did not, however, have much power over her husband. In her efforts, when she could find the time, Barbara nagged Taylor, pleading with him to "behave himself." Wasn't it rather childish risking his life on the roads and in the air? What was the purpose? Defying life is a childish game, she tried to convince him. Was he running *to* or *from* something? But why? If Cooper was frustrated over his love life and Gable was devastated because of Lombard's death, what was Bob's reason for trying to destroy himself? Her protests went unheeded.

MGM finally stepped in and demanded Gable sell his motorcycle. "What the hell," he said to Taylor. "Let's go huntin' up Oregon way!"

Barbara was torn between having her husband in danger away from home or in danger near home. He had calmed down on his motorcycle since MGM gave him warning so Barbara, in motherly fashion, bought him a much more expensive one. She hoped he'd stay home and enjoy it. Besides, she could well afford the best. In 1944 Barbara Stanwyck had graduated to the position of highest-salaried woman in the United States—$323,333.

Barbara Stanwyck as she appeared in
her Broadway stage hit, *Burlesque* (1927).

KING FEATURES

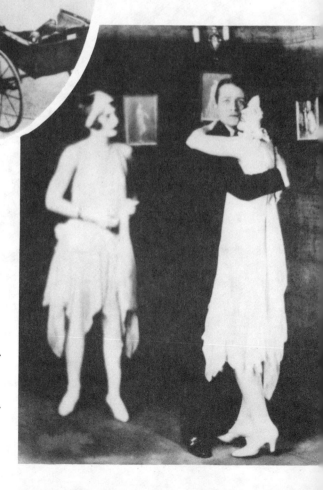

Barbara when she was still Ruby Stevens, with brother Malcolm Byron. She was the toughest kid on her Brooklyn block.

Rare stage photo of Barbara and lover Rex Cherryman in *The Noose* (1926). Cherryman died two years after this photo was taken.

A nautical publicity still from *Shopworn*
(1932). MOVIE STAR NEWS

Frank Fay, the Irish Broadway vaudevillian, husband number one. It was a battle royale over whose career was to take precedence: Fay's on Broadway in New York City, or Barbara's in Hollywood?
MOVIE STAR NEWS

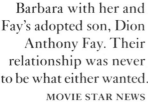

Barbara with her and Fay's adopted son, Dion Anthony Fay. Their relationship was never to be what either wanted.
MOVIE STAR NEWS

Top, left: working with Hollywood greats such as Gary Cooper always brought out the best in Barbara—and them; here in *Meet John Doe.*
Top, right: the tearjerker of all time—*Stella Dallas*—with Anne Shirley. Barbara's first Oscar nomination—and loss. Barbara: "I should have won." *Bottom, left:* testifying in the bitter custody battle with Fay over Dion. KING FEATURES

Romance blossoms—on and off the screen.
Barbara's first film with Robert Taylor, *His
Brother's Wife* (1936). He was to become husband
number two—and the man she would love for the
rest of her life, even after their divorce.

By the time of
This Is My Affair (1937),
the public couldn't get
enough of Barbara and
Taylor's love affair.
They were in all the
fan magazines.

"Off to Navy Service," reads the original caption for this photo. "Wife Barbara Stanwyck walks with Lieutenant Robert Taylor to the car as the screen star leaves for active Navy duty."

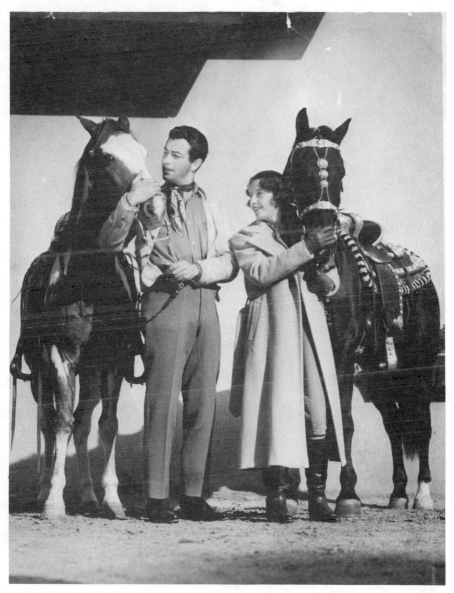

For the press corps, the Taylors were the perfect Hollywood couple: gorgeous and in love. *Opposite, above:* Barbara gives a gallant try for the camera on one of Bob's motorcycles (she loathed them). *Opposite, below:* inviting the camera into their home. *Above:* although Barbara was terrified of motorcycles she had horses under her grip.

(Uncle) Buck Mack, Barbara, and Bob

William Holden came on strong in *Golden Boy* (1939), the movie that made him a star. But without Barbara's help and influence with studio bigwigs, they would have dumped him. MOVIE STAR NEWS

Other stars sniffed at *Lady of Burlesque*
(1943), but Barbara had great fun making it.

As Phyllis Dietrichson, the woman every man would kill for, in *Double Indemnity* (1944), Barbara earned her third Oscar nomination.

During the forties, Barbara acted in a lot of radio drama (as did many other film stars). Here with "The Prudential Family Hour of Stars." *Clockwise from top, left:* Gregory Peck, Robert Taylor, Ray Milland, Bette Davis, Ginger Rogers, and Barbara.

In *Sorry, Wrong Number* (1948) Barbara played a bed-ridden wife who suspected her husband of plotting to murder her. Her bravura performance earned her a fourth Oscar nomination.

Rare photo of Babs with her hair down. She's checking her script on the set of *Titanic* (1953). KING FEATURES

Hollywood's perfect marriage started showing its cracks when Bob came up against the irresistible Lana Turner in *Johnny Eager* (1941).

The now *very* divorced couple of Barbara and Bob reteamed, much to their chagrin, in *The Night Walker* (1965), a William Castle fright opus.

The Queen: as tough and beautiful as ever.
In her Emmy Award–winning performance in
The Thorn Birds (1982).

Five

While Taylor was in the navy, Barbara went ahead and purchased a three-bedroom house in Beverly Hills. Once he returned, very few friends were invited to see it and those who did said, "Listening to Barbara yelling at Bob and watching him take it wasn't very pleasant. He never fought back."

Tom Purvis came to Los Angeles from his home in Illinois, but stayed at a hotel. Barbara's famous statement, "Don't ever want to be a houseguest and don't ever want a houseguest!" was taken quite literally and she was glad that it was.

In an interview regarding her marriage she said, "Bob is a great sleeper while I sit up and read a book. He naps in the afternoon. These naps he calls 'resting his eyes.' He never broke away from Nebraska and still has a sense of belonging there. He's likely to stay up in his plane and never come down. He can do anything a bird can but sit on a barbed wire fence."

In *The Strange Love of Martha Ivers*, Stanwyck portrayed another cold-blooded murderess, but this one makes Phyllis Dietrichson look like a nun. As Martha, she kills her aunt and inherits a fortune, marries Kirk Douglas, who knows the truth, and they have an innocent man put to death. He becomes an alcoholic and she becomes a "loose woman" before falling in love with Van Heflin who, she hopes, will kill Douglas. In the end, she and Douglas commit suicide. It was a juicy role she was really able to sink her teeth into—and the critics loved it.

Never one to look back for even a moment, Barbara was anxious to get the part of Dominique in the film version of Ayn Rand's best-selling novel *Fountainhead*. There were very few good roles, she explained and, like the character Stella Dallas, she fought very hard and suggested Humphrey Bogart as her costar. They had not exactly become friends in *The Two Mrs. Carrolls*, but she admired his acting. Whether Bogart was ever considered isn't certain, but Gary Cooper was signed for the lead. And the actress whom he would fall in love with, Patricia Neal, got the part of Dominique.

According to director King Vidor, Barbara wasn't considered because she had no sex appeal. Stanwyck was surely disappointed. She felt snubbed and hurt—no woman likes to be told she has no sex appeal.

Her very next film, *California*, was her first color film, an outdoor epic that was a challenge for Barbara because color added a new dimension to moviemaking. This otherwise unexceptional Western with Ray Milland was more "product" than anything else.

In *Cry Wolf* Barbara costarred with Errol Flynn, who, like Bogie in *The Two Mrs. Carrolls*, plays an insane killer. She had a lot to do—both acting and stunt work—and it's a pretty solid thriller, although not as good as it could have been if it had had a stronger script with more depth. But it was fun for all concerned and still popular.

The Other Love was a sensitive movie about a fatally ill woman who falls in love with her doctor, played by David

Niven. When she learns the truth about her health, she runs off to Monte Carlo for a fling. In the end she marries the kind doctor and lives out her final days peacefully with the man she loves.

All of these 1947 movies were not outstanding, but they were all good enough to keep her in favorable reviews and never lacking for decent scripts.

In February 1947 the Taylors took a rare vacation abroad. Much of their trip to Europe was highly publicized, but the press did not report that the purpose of the three weeks away from Hollywood was to mend their bad marriage. One of Barbara's friends said, "She desperately wanted to find a way to keep Bob. His eyes were roving in her presence these days without his realizing it because he would never do it otherwise. Pretty young girls were naturally attracted to him wherever he went and he returned their glances. How Barbara was going to keep him was anyone's guess because it was hopeless as far as everyone else was concerned. But they went to Europe supposedly to see what it was like to be together since they were separated by their careers most of the time. Barbara was terrified of traveling, and we thought it was quite brave of her to take the long trip until word got out that one of her films, *The Other Love*, was going to premiere in London. As much as she loved Bob, Barbara would have found another way to be with him alone unless somewhere along the line her career was involved."

They arrived in Paris for sightseeing and relaxation before going to England. They had reserved a grand suite at the Hotel George V. Oddly no reporter saw them arrive in France or at their hotel. The Taylors literally disappeared.

Four days after their arrival in Paris, Barbara was reported to be staying at the American Hospital in Neuilly. When the press inquired about the illness, the hospital staff said she had a cold.

Reporters surmised she had been taken ill on the ship

and slipped away in an ambulance unnoticed. Doctors would not give any details other than, "There was not adequate heat at the hotel and Miss Stanwyck decided to stay at the hospital rather than risk pneumonia."

Reporters wanted to know where Robert Taylor was.

The press agent said Taylor was in Paris and that his wife met him "for dinner there occasionally," but returned to her hospital bed to sleep.

There was little gossip in Hollywood about this arrangement because the Taylors fought constantly when they were together for any length of time, and four days on a ship might have been too much. Barbara was good at "dishing it out," but crumbled on the rare occasions she got the same in return—especially from Bob. Friends were concerned for her health, but it was confirmed she had only a slight cold.

How could a slight cold separate a couple who were on vacation just to be together? It is remarkable that reporters did not build up this unusual situation, but MGM protected Taylor at all costs and under all circumstances. The press hung around the hotel and the hospital trying to gather more information. One reporter who spoke only French wondered why Stanwyck, who supposedly found the hotel too cold, did not snuggle up to her husband for warmth.

Before the press could find enough evidence that Barbara and Bob were having serious problems and print the proof in black and white, the Taylors were seen at the Follies-Bergère.

Apparently Barbara soon felt better because she agreed to accompany Bob to Holland, Belgium, and England. There was very little publicity until they arrived in London to attend the premier of *The Other Love* in Leicester Square, where they were mobbed by five thousand fans. Police had to hoist them on their shoulders. Stanwyck was terrified, unlike Taylor who was accustomed to such enthusiastic crowds. "Hell, I've been stripped down to my shorts," he laughed. "I've had to walk down fire escapes without my shoes, salute an admiral with a regulation tie cut off by some young kid, and ride in freight elevators with white tie and tails."

Taylor did, however, get a black eye at the London premiere and the morning papers printed MOB SHINES ROBERT TAYLOR.

Friends back home wanted to know: "Since when is Barbara a mob?"

Stanwyck had not enjoyed the trip abroad. She considered the nightclubs in Paris too risqué; she refused to buy even one piece of clothing made by French designers because, "I think American women who go to Paris for clothes are wrong. Our designers managed very well during the war with inferior material and we should support our country." When asked about the mob in London she said, "I was totally overwhelmed and shocked at first until I realized they meant well."

Stanwyck told anyone who wanted to listen that she much preferred America and would be glad to get home. Taylor said very little, but he was happier when the USS *America* landed in New York than she was. It had been a boring trip for him and he wondered why he had taken the vacation in the first place. He missed his cronies and his airplane and his freedom. Not bothering to smile for photographers, his boredom was apparent. Barbara was terrified of traveling even with Bob and, once she arrived at a destination, all she did was worry about the trip back. Besides, she was in demand in Hollywood. Scripts were waiting to be read and cameras ready to roll. There was work to do.

Helen Ferguson, their press agent—and Barbara's best friend—met them in New York and insisted they attend the theater. "Maurice Chevalier is a smash and tickets are hard to get." The Taylors would have preferred leaving for California immediately, but they did not want to disappoint Helen.

When the curtain went down on the Chevalier show, an usher came over to extend an invitation backstage. Barbara and Bob were sensitive about such things and never would go backstage without a personal invitation, but Helen insisted. "Let's not insult Mr. Chevalier!"

They waited endlessly in the dressing room. Barbara wanted to leave and Bob started for the door, but Helen urged them to stay just a few minutes more. Chevalier appeared and ignored them completely. Barbara turned purple and began to cry. Bob took her by the arm and led her out into the street to hail a cab. All the way back to the hotel he ranted and raved while Barbara trembled with shock. Neither had ever been so embarrassed.

The last insult on their stay in New York was a reporter's question: "Are you going to see Frank Fay in *Harvey*, Miss Stanwyck?"

"Hardly!" she sneered.

The Taylors took the train to Chicago. Bob's private plane was waiting for him there, but Barbara insisted she continue by rail. Taylor flew on ahead and met her at the station. Again she told reporters in Los Angeles that she was "so relieved to be home!" But home to Taylor was just another place to hang his hat until he could make arrangements for another fishing or hunting trip.

In *B. F.'s Daughter*, with Charles Coburn and Van Heflin, Barbara cut her shoulder-length hair to keep up with the latest style. MGM's hairdresser insisted Barbara touch up and hide streaks of white hair on both sides of her forehead. Although photographs were touched-up, Barbara refused to do that to her hair. Not only did the studios beg her to submit to dye, so did her close friends. "I'm forty-one," she laughed. "So what? If I'm destined to have prematurely white hair, so be it. I have no intention of lying about my age nor do I have any intention of going through that tedious job of having my hair colored every week. I couldn't go through that."

During the production of the classic *Sorry, Wrong Number*, Stanwyck's hair turned entirely white. *Life* magazine described her part, played mostly in bed, as "the most extended emotional jag in recent movie history." It was a choice role and Barbara was eager to do it, but she confessed it was exhausting.

"For twelve straight days I had to be on an emotional high, playing a bedridden woman and knowing someone is going to murder me. I lived the role, but can you imagine how hard it was to leave the studio each night in a high state of anxiety and terror, go home to eat and sleep and get up the next day to start all over again?"

It was difficult for Stanwyck to "come down" when she left the studio and then get "emotionally tied-up" at nine the next morning. She obviously lived this role of the neurotic lady dialing the telephone frantically for help. She cleverly asked director Anatole Litvak if he could arrange the filming schedule so that she could do the terrifying scenes consecutively, and he complied, thus contributing to both the cinematic effect and emotional drain.

All the critics praised *Sorry, Wrong Number*.

Cue magazine said, "For sheer, unadulterated terror there have been few films in recent years to match the quivering fright of *Sorry, Wrong Number*—and few performances to equal the hysteria-ridden picture of a woman doomed, as portrayed by Barbara Stanwyck.

"Miss Stanwyck gives one of the finest performances of her career—a carefully calculated, skillfully integrated picture of developing psychological terror that provides a filmic highlight of the year."

Barbara admitted being worried about this role—the hysteria compacted into twelve days. But she was nominated for another Academy Award—her fourth.

"I will not win the award this year for best actress," she

told one reporter, "because I haven't been nominated enough. Only been nominated four times! It all depends on my work in 1949. If I get nominated next year, they'll have to give me the door prize, won't they? At least the bride should throw me the bouquet."

On another occasion Barbara sighed, "Not that I wouldn't like to have an Oscar, but I've lost three times before and it's hard to get your expectations up and not win. It's bad luck to discuss it. Besides, I feel Olivia de Havilland really deserves it for *The Snake Pit.*"

Her competition was not as keen as in previous years: Irene Dunne in *I Remember Mama*, Jane Wyman in *Johnny Belinda*, Ingrid Bergman in *Joan of Arc*, and Olivia de Havilland.

Barbara went to the Academy Award ceremonies in a frustrated mood, knowing her peers had nominated her four times and she had yet to grasp that statue—her one unattained goal in life.

She lost to Jane Wyman, who, as a deaf mute, did not have to say any lines for *Johnny Belinda* and had to compensate with sensitive acting.

Taylor, still in a mild slump, was not being hounded for interviews these days, but during one of the few he gave did not sound happy. "I was better off financially when I was drawing a lieutenant's pay than before or after the war. Barbara and I were left with $5,000 a year between us when I was earning comparatively nothing. She was able to divide her income between us for taxation. But," he sighed. "I guess she'd rather have me home and pay."

Trying to take his monotonous life in stride, Taylor took to the skies and highways, the streams and the woods. The trip to Europe had been a dismal failure, but that was behind him. They were both exhausted from trying and failing and then trying and politely getting along for a little while. Taylor told a friend, "I don't know why the hell people think they can save a marriage by getting on a boat for a change of scenery when the change of scenery is each other."

Barbara, despite her hectic schedule, was taking a solid look at her marriage, and, oddly, her hair figured in her deliberations. Her close friends begged her to touch up her white hair, but she exclaimed that it was quite stunning and nature's choice. But the braver ones tried seriously to convince her: "You don't want to look more like Bob's mother every day, do you? No one is suggesting that you try to look younger than you really are, but why allow yourself to look older than you are?"

Still Barbara would not budge. If Bob were going to love her, it would be for what she was inside and how much they meant to each other, not because of a few bottles of hair dye.

She was also urged to be a "good sport" with Taylor. "Try to share some of his hobbies even if it kills you," friends said.

She referred to his plane—named *Missy* after her nickname—as "the Crate" and had yet to go near it. "He flew the Crate from Los Angeles to New Orleans and back by way of Detroit just to test a new plane radio!" she said with a tone of resentment.

But the time had come, however, for Barbara to make some long-overdue sacrifices for Bob and for her marriage. One morning she said to Bob, "It looks like a clear day and you probably won't hit any mountains, right?" For the first time in years, Taylor's eyes lit up in her company. He telephoned a dozen friends to tell them the Queen was actually going up in his plane!

The ride to the airport was a quiet one. When she spotted the plane, she began trembling, but she got aboard without too much hesitation. In the air she was terrified, grabbing the seat with both hands and hanging on for dear life. She closed her eyes and remained silent. When they landed in Palm Springs an hour later, she was pale and sick.

Bob considered this the greatest gift she had ever given him. He talked about it for weeks. Seeing how his attitude had changed, she attempted to ride a motorcycle while reporters took pictures. She appeared as if she were about to take off for the moon instead of a jaunt around the block. Whether she even got the engine started isn't known. It was apparent she was doing everything possible to please Bob.

She volunteered to go on a hunting and camping trip with Bob, Gary Cooper and Ernest Hemingway. Barbara had worked with Cooper and they admired each other professionally, but he was a different man in the woods and wasn't interested in discussing the movie business. Taylor was impressed with Hemingway, but Hemingway wasn't impressed with Taylor. Barbara wasn't impressed at all. When she got back home, her only comment was, "Never again!"

Barbara was candid about Bob's hobbies. "I never could understand how he could spend hours and days planning a fishing trip, get all enthused, and run out of the house with a truckload of gear only to come back and leave dozens of dead fish on the back porch. Rarely did he cook them. The smell was beyond description. All that planning for nothing except a stink."

Taylor's sleeping bags and camping equipment were always ready to go. Then Barbara would announce she had time off, and Bob, feeling obligated to stay home, cleaned his guns and stared longingly out the window. He later admitted it would have been better all around if he *had* packed up early and left, doing as he pleased rather than trying to pacify Barbara—and holding back his resentment.

His hunting buddies were actually afraid to call him about a jaunt and reluctant to bring up the subject when

Barbara was in the room. She didn't especially like their conversations, which excluded her, and it annoyed her to see Bob's beaming face when he was engrossed in a gab session about sports. Tom Purvis came out from Illinois for a visit and stayed at a hotel. "Barbara didn't like me, so I didn't like Barbara," Purvis said. "Understand we didn't know each other except for one or two brief encounters, but I was Bob's navy buddy and she was jealous. I felt kind of sorry for him because he put me up in a suite in the best hotel to make up for the lack of hospitality on Barbara's part—though he never put it to me that way. He knew that I knew. I did not even see half of the rooms in my suite, but Bob paid for everything."

Taylor's fishing and hunting buddies were not all as famous as John Wayne, Robert Stack, and Clark Gable, but regardless of who they were, Barbara made it clear to Taylor she preferred that they did not come to their home. Occasionally she gave in for a party, but the topic of conversation could not be guns, fishing rods, or airplanes—"by special request." Not only was it boring for Barbara, it was irritating.

One evening the Taylors entertained a variety of friends at their home and Barbara retired early, leaving Bob and his cronies alone. John Wayne remembered it well: "One tall tale led to another and time passed with lies about the big fish we caught and the bears who sniffed our sleeping bags while we were in 'em and about the guns we were adding to our collection. The booze and beer flowed. Just a bunch of guys gettin' drunk and havin' a good time, until *she* appeared at the top of the stairs in her nightgown and yelled at Bob. 'Get up here now!' she shouted and told him to join her in bed. I can't repeat what else she said but it had to do with sex and what she wanted him to do. Hell, this story got around Hollywood faster than a tornado. I didn't give a good goddamn what she said. Taylor was the host as far as I was concerned, but it was so humiliating for Bob that we all went home. He took it—in front of all those guys, by God. I might have told her where a wife belongs and how a real lady should act and talk. I wanted to tell her myself—face to face—nightgown and all, but why add to Bob's problems? He had to live with her, I didn't."

Dion Fay, who might have appreciated some scolding from his mother, rarely saw or spoke to her. For ten years he was ignored—in and out of boarding schools and away at camp during the summer vacations. Then one day he was thrilled to find out she was paying him a visit. There was no hug or kiss or words of affection. Barbara stated in businesslike fashion that she could no longer tolerate his bad grades. "I'm sending you east to Culver Military Academy in Indiana," Barbara announced coldly. "They'll shape you up!"

That was the last time Dion saw his mother for another four years. During his summer vacations he was provided with transportation from Indiana to California, but not to the Taylor house in Beverly Hills. Barbara paid his room and board at the home of two elderly women in the Los Angeles area, but Dion was instructed not to visit his mother or attempt to see her.

Taylor said Dion begged to come home many times, but never dared arrive without an invitation. "Except for bad grades, he was not a bad kid. After all, he hadn't been home since he was five years old. He was overweight and not the cutest boy in town, which Dion claimed was the reason his mother didn't want him around. It was tough on the kid to be told he was to forget Barbara was his mother because she wanted nothing more to do with him. That was the message he got from his Uncle Buck [Buck Mack], not from his mother.

"Dion was not athletic. I tried to teach him tennis and a little golf, but he wasn't interested. It was hard to reach the kid because he saw nothing of his mother and father and had no personal affection, attention, or direction. I did not think it was my place to interfere, so I stayed out of it—completely."

Reporters wanted to know about Dion, but Helen Ferguson said that Barbara Stanwyck's personal life was exactly that—personal. "It was a very difficult time for Barbara from 1946 on," Helen reflected. "Her marriage was in serious trouble and her movies were not to her liking. This was not the time to have Dion around."

Six

When Taylor had returned from the navy, he found himself with two mothers, though he was not aware of this. He loved Barbara, but not the way a man loves a wife. He began to compare Barbara to his own mother, who Bob felt was a paradigm regardless of her shortcomings and early senility. Returning to Hollywood after the war was one of the most depressing and confused times in Taylor's life. Aside from his marital problems, it would take five years for him to regain his superstar status.

The final blow was his inability to perform with Barbara in bed. "I have a prostate problem," he lied, trying to stall for time. But when Bob failed to mention seeing a doctor and ignored her suggestions about a cure for this problem, Barbara became suspicious. If a man wasn't satisfied at home, he must be going elsewhere. There was, however, no evidence that he was seeing other women. Not even a rumor. Thinking it over logically, there was only one explanation. If Bob wasn't sleeping with her and if he wasn't sleeping with another woman, he had to be a

homosexual. The more she thought about it, the more
sense it made. There was the early gossip about the pretty
boy image, but then Bob had been normal before going
into the navy. Still, when he came home, Ralph Couser
was with him. They worked together at MGM, flew *Missy*
everywhere together and shared other mutual interests.
And Ralph was one of the few who dared call the house.

Taylor ignored her insinuations because he knew the
frustration of not sharing his bed with him was the source
of her ire. He was afraid to try again because he was terrified of not being able to perform. It was humiliating to
him and frustrating to her. More accusations and more
fighting.

She confronted Taylor about his "affair" with Couser.
Bob said nothing. It was too degrading for any response.
His apparent indifference enraged Barbara, who tried another approach. Whenever Couser telephoned, Barbara
would yell, "Hey, Bob, your wife wants to talk to you!"

Taylor took it and much more.

Convinced he was losing his virility or perhaps his interest in women, Bob went to a psychologist. The doctor
had known Bob for many years on a social basis and was
well acquainted with his mother and Barbara.

"Bob was terribly upset," the doctor said. "When he
was a little boy, his mother dressed him up in frilly
clothes and fawned over his gorgeous looks. Then Hollywood labeled him pretty boy and forced him to prove he
was all man. The press and the public called him everything but a homosexual, though his fan mail spelled it out.
Baring his chest in 1937 to prove he had hair and finding
this revealing photo on the front pages of every newspaper in the world with the headlines TAYLOR BARES CHEST
TO PROVE HE-NESS was a dreadful experience for a young
man. So silly, but that was the code in 1937. Bob never
forgot that. So, when Barbara accused him of being gay,
Taylor actually believed he was.

"Upsetting him more was his eagerness to make his marriage work. He did not want to be just another movie star getting just another divorce. The big question was what to do now that he could not get aroused by her.

"We had to eliminate the homosexual stigma first, so I asked him if he had ever been attracted to men. I thought he was going to kill me! So, of course, my next question was whether he had been attracted to any women lately. He said, 'I get a goddamn hot sensation in my groin when I see a sexy looking dame!'

"I told him a couple of things straight from the shoulder both as a friend and as a doctor. He was not queer. I was sure of that. Then I explained the concept of his having two mothers. A man does not get aroused by his mother in bed. Taking it from there, it was up to him—and him alone—to prove that he was *not* a homosexual and the only way to do that was to go out and get laid!

"My final suggestion was not to worry about his marriage until he found the much-needed confidence in himself—above all."

The doctor said it was not as easy as one might think for a famous movie actor to "go out and get laid"—"especially Bob because he was a romantic guy and he had to be attracted to a woman. Call girls were out. MGM had a stable at one time to keep their male stars happy and clean, but this luxury no longer existed. However, I knew that Bob felt better knowing there was nothing wrong with him and understanding the psychology of having two mothers, one of them his wife. He would find a way."

Ironically Bob's costar in his next movie, *The Bribe*, was the beautiful and sensual Ava Gardner. She was close to his friend Clark Gable and pleasant to be with—understanding, witty, direct, and sexy. Bob enjoyed her company and they met occasionally—sometimes at Ruth's house, much to his mother's distress. Finally she confronted him about it and Taylor asked, "Would you rather I go to a motel where I might be recognized,

Mother?" Ruth made it a little more convenient for Bob
and Ava from then on.

Taylor finally knew the answer. He certainly was not
homosexual but there was nothing he could do when he
tried to make it with Barbara. With all the other burdens,
this ultimate lack of closeness marked the bitter end. The
decline was rapid from then on.

Then their careers did a turnabout. Barbara's movies
were going from bad to worse in 1949 and 1950. *The Lady
Gambles* with Robert Preston was fair, and *East Side,
West Side* with Van Heflin was not much better. This
film is best known for the presence of a nervous newcomer, actress Nancy Davis, who was making her third
appearance on the screen. Director Mervyn LeRoy introduced her to an actor at Warner Brothers—Ronald Reagan—and the rest of this story is far more interesting than
East Side, West Side.

Her costar in her next film, *The File on Thelma Jor-
dan*, was the always interesting and perceptive Wendell
Corey. This was a fine and subtle example of film noir
directed by Robert Siodmak, but a box office bomb nonetheless. By now Stanwyck knew she was in a slump, but
without a good, fresh script on the horizon, there was little she could do. *No Man of Her Own* with John Lund
did nothing to bring cheers from the critics, though Stanwyck was rarely panned. During her entire career she
never received unqualified praise from critics. For example: Winston Burdett: "Stanwyck has no emotion."
Howard Barnes: "She's wooden." Archer Winsten, who
did not like her looks or her acting.

Barbara Stanwyck always gave the best performance
possible despite bad scripts and weak costars. Her efforts
were visible and critics gave her credit for at least that
much. In 1949 she was worked harder than ever trying to
maintain her sanity and ease the heavy burden on her
heart—Robert Taylor.

The Furies with Walter Huston was fair enough. This

Western was a change of pace and was good for Stan-wyck, as she had been playing long-suffering women in her last few films. In *The Furies* she portrayed a kind of grown-up Annie Oakley with a constant flow of abundant energy. Huston died shortly after completion of the movie, and since he and Barbara had been very close, she felt his loss deeply.

She filmed *To Please a Lady* with Clark Gable her co-star of twenty years previous in *Night Nurse*. It was a fast-moving and clever film about a newspaper columnist and a racing driver. Gable, however, was not a compatible screen mate because she did not resemble the type of woman he might try to seduce. Nor was Gable her kind of guy as were Fonda and Cooper. Overall *To Please a Lady* was a run-of-the-mill motion picture that got neither good nor bad reviews.

Taylor, meanwhile, was on his way to bigger and better things. He called Purvis in Illinois to tell him he was "heading for England to do a picture with a little girl I think might be something one day. Think her name is Elizabeth, but I know we have Taylor in common."

In *The Conspirator* Robert Taylor gave seventeen-year-old Elizabeth Taylor her first screen kiss. She was frightened and he thought that cute until he saw the newspaper headlines the next day. Taylor called his agent in Hollywood: "Don't you think this first-kiss business is going a little too far? Makes me feel like a damn ass, and why tease a little girl like that?"

Elizabeth was in heaven after the kiss. She cooed and sighed: "Today I grew up. No one can say I am a child in this picture, because I am playing Robert Taylor's wife! He is just as wonderful as everyone in Hollywood told me he was. I have to admit I did get nervous when he took me in his arms and made love to me, but the director said I shouldn't be upset."

Elizabeth Taylor had been studying algebra in the little

studio schoolroom near the set. When the class was dismissed, she rushed out the door, stood for a moment while
she dabbed her nose with a powder puff and put some
perfume behind her ears. After the love scene she walked
in a daze back to her dressing room and with childish ec-
stasy said to her hairdresser: "I've just been kissed by
Robert Taylor. Do you know he's almost forty years old?
And that he said I was talented? But he did have to teach
me how to powder down my lips."

As the filming progressed, however, both Taylors
changed their minds about each other. Bob began to take
notice of "that little girl." He commented: "For God's
sake, she was stacked! I didn't realize it until she appeared
on the set in a negligee. She was just a child, but I
couldn't help myself.

"It wouldn't have been so bad," he continued, "if they
shot the scene with me sitting down, but I spent the entire
day in that condition. Finally I spoke to the cameraman
and he aimed the lens from my waist up!"

Elizabeth was getting annoyed at Bob's "advances."
She claims he almost broke her back as he bent her over a
bannister with an overzealous—and unnecessary—kiss.
She later said Bob was responsible for her chronic back
problems for the rest of her life, but it is common knowledge that when she was twelve years old, during the filming of *National Velvet,* she fell off a horse and severely
injured her back.

Elizabeth Taylor began *The Conspirator* in awe of
Robert Taylor and ended the film despising him.

Bob said, "Always had my eye on her. A few years later
we were together again in *Ivanhoe,* but she was chasing
after Michael Wilding and only had eyes for him."

Taylor's infatuation with Elizabeth was obvious and
the news leaked out. Barbara took the stories with a shrug
and could not be bothered discussing the matter.

After Taylor's next two films, which were made in

Hollywood, MGM gave him the lead in *Quo Vadis:* with estimated production costs of over $7 million, it was the highest-budgeted movie in film history at the time. (*Gone With the Wind* had carried a cost of $4 million.) *Quo Vadis* was scheduled for six months of filming at the huge Cinecittà studios—eight miles outside Rome—which covered 148 acres and nine big sound stages.

While plans were being made, the Stanwyck—Taylor marriage glided through nothingness, not the subject of much gossip or speculation. It had lasted longer than Hollywood thought possible. MGM cleverly painted a calm picture, and Helen Ferguson's articles about the "perfect couple" depicted moonlight and roses. Both Barbara and Bob were dignified in their apartness and never said an unkind word about each other. He repeated his admiration for her and she was always sympathetic about his uphill fight to regain popularity as a star after the war.

She talked openly about her own slump. "I'll murder—and have done so—or take falls and have done so. I thrive on work. I get more tired trying to find something to do when I'm not working." When asked about the critics who were not thrilled with her last few pictures, Barbara said, "They don't have the control everyone thinks they have. If they did, we would all have been out of work a long time ago."

When asked about her future plans she replied, "It would be nice to do a comedy."

Stanwyck still maintained her independence and was not under contract to one studio. The contract system was fading anyway, as television captured the public's imagination, and in response Hollywood tried to improve the scope and quality of its pictures. One such film was *Quo Vadis.*

Tom Purvis flew to Rome to spend a few weeks with Taylor.

"We lived like kings," Purvis said. "Bob had a chef and a chauffeur. We went to the little out-of-the-way restaurants and ate stuff we never knew existed. One night we were relaxing in his apartment. A girl called from the lobby and said she was coming up, but he wanted me to stay while she was there. Bob told me she was an aspiring actress and it might give the wrong impression if he were alone with her. At the time I was sure there was nothing going on between them. Seemed to me it was the usual crush-on-a-movie-star thing or maybe she thought he could get her into the movies."

Despite Taylor's precaution that night, the gossip columnists were unanimous in their assessment that he was "fooling around" with other women in Rome. Rumors persisted until finally only one woman was identified—a bit player, Lia De Leo. Barbara put up a good front at first. In an interview with Louella Parsons she admitted there had been some unhappiness in her marriage. "It began when he bought that airplane," she said, "and when I realized he was always on some kind of hunting or fishing trip with his friends, I asked Bob if he wanted me to make fewer movies and he insisted I continue working."

Louella wanted to know how she felt about Bob's being in Italy for six months. "I'm lonely for him," Barbara responded. "I am planning to spend a few months with him in Rome. When you have been married happily for ten years, you miss not seeing him around—even with a backyard littered with fish and airplane parts!"

Cheerfully Barbara said she planned to visit friends in Paris and London first because it was dreadfully hot in Rome and besides, "Bob was so busy with *Quo Vadis*."

Barbara, who was accustomed to gossip about her husband, usually ignored exaggerated tales, but the stories about Lia De Leo, she learned from reliable sources, were true.

Helen Ferguson explained, "Barbara was terrified of flying. She would rather face a herd of wild horses barehanded and alone, but one night she called me and announced, 'I'm going to Rome and you're going with me!' So I began packing. This was the biggest and bravest decision Barbara had ever made. It *had* to be important. Otherwise she never would have faced that long plane trip."

Stanwyck had been negotiating to make a film in London. The script was being written exclusively for her. Her original plans to travel by boat to England, make the movie, surprise Bob in Rome, return to London for retakes and sail back to New York with him were forgotten. The threat of Lia De Leo changed all that.

MGM announced that Barbara Stanwyck was taking a vacation to be with Taylor for six weeks, and she "eagerly awaited the chance to sightsee in such a beautiful country."

Helen Ferguson said Barbara put up a magnificent front. "She was sick and afraid on the flight to Rome. Not only was sitting on the plane tearing her nerves to shreds, but the realization that her husband was openly having an affair at the destination broke her heart. But Bob was most thoughtful and had arranged elegant and comfortable accommodations. He knew, for instance, that it was difficult to obtain various brands of makeup, tissues, and so forth, but he made sure we had everything."

The press watched the Taylors carefully. MGM officials made certain there was no adverse publicity and concentrated on Bob showing Barbara the traditional sights of Rome. Helen tried to cover up tension by emphasizing how happy Barbara was to see her husband and that Bob was "tickled pink" to have her in Rome.

But the inevitable happened. Barbara wanted to know what had been going on. Was he playing around with other women? Or was he having an affair with one in par-

ticular? Rumors do not persist unless there is some truth
to them. She had heard from *very* reliable sources that he
was spending a lot of time with this Lia and, if so, what
did this mean?

Bob denied the seriousness of any relationship. Yes, he
had some good times sharing dinner and a few dances,
swimming or taking an occasional drive in the country.
He was under a great deal of pressure and wasn't going to
lock himself in his spacious apartment every night.

Barbara did not accept these answers. After each innocent explanation, she just repeated the question: "What's
going on and who is Lia De Leo?"

The psychologist who had helped Taylor through his
fear of homosexuality has commented on this confronta-
tion: "Bob's personality was remarkable. He could take a
beating and never speak up. Eventually everyone has a
breaking point if they are nagged and questioned repeatedly. Bob reached that point with Barbara in Rome. She
accused him of having affairs with several women and
when he did not react, she concentrated on Lia De Leo—
over and over—but still Bob remained silent. Barbara
threatened divorce and admitted later this was only an attempt to frighten him. Then she ripped into his affair
with Lia, and Taylor exploded: 'At least I can get it up
with her!' "

Barbara said she wanted a divorce and stormed out of
Rome.

It took only nine words to almost destroy Barbara
Stanwyck. Sick and heartbroken, she returned to Hollywood with Helen Ferguson. Plans for her special movie in
London were canceled. She told the producer, "My whole
life has fallen apart. I cannot think of anything else right
now. Filing for divorce will take everything out of me, but
it has to be done."

In September 1950 she sailed on the Queen Elizabeth
and bravely faced reporters. "Rome wasn't great," she

said. "They were shooting scenes with lions and bulls and everything smelled awful."

One reporter asked about Taylor. "Being with Bob is always wonderful," she said, managing a weak smile.

In November 1950 Taylor completed *Quo Vadis* and was preparing to leave his apartment for the airport. He had heard little from Barbara since her departure almost three months ago, and although he tried to keep his name out of the newspapers to avoid hurting her further, he knew the marriage was over. Their marriage had lasted ten years, a long time by Hollywood standards. This, after all, was an important element in his clean and wholesome image.

When he appeared in the lobby of his apartment building in Rome with his luggage, Lia was waiting for him. Taylor was taken by surprise when she flung herself into his arms. She covered his face with loving kisses—and the cameras clicked.

Bob smiled, but gently pushed her away and hurried to his limousine. Lia did not follow him, but she was ready to make a statement to reporters she had cleverly brought with her to Bob's apartment.

Lia said she was the former wife of the king's attorney. Now she was "Robert Taylor's big love"—and had been throughout the filming of *Quo Vadis*. "He is tired of her [Barbara] and he told me so," she said.

Taylor refused comment at the airport and returned to Hollywood where pictures of him and Lia were front-page news. He ignored the reporters and went home.

Newspapers announced that the Taylors had separated, but within a few days after Bob's arrival in Hollywood, they announced they were going to San Francisco together. Later it was revealed that Taylor entered the hospital there to be operated on for the removal of a double hernia. Barbara remained with him and told Louella Parsons, "Those hours he was on the operating table were the worst I have ever spent in my life."

Louella asked tactfully what their future plans were. Barbara said they were going on a three-month vacation together, but instead he went to Palm Springs alone, and Barbara went into hiding at the home of friends in Hollywood.

The divorce announcement was made on December 16, 1950, through their press agent, Helen Ferguson, who broke down in tears, handed the paper to Howard Strickling, head of MGM publicity. Bob had asked Howard to "be very gentle with Helen during this time."

The Taylors issued a joint statement.

> In the past few years, because of professional requirements, we have been separated just too often and too long. Our sincere and continued efforts to maintain our marriage have failed. We are deeply disappointed that we could not solve our problems. We really tried. We unhappily and reluctantly admit that we have denied to even our closest friends because we wanted to work things out together in as much privacy as possible. There will be a California divorce. Neither of us has any other romantic interest whatsoever.

In an interview a reporter mentioned to Barbara that her marriage to Bob was often pointed to as the one perfect example that two famous film stars could have separate careers and a happy marriage, too.

"That was the damn trouble!" Barbara cried. "Separate careers! We have been separated just too often and too long. I have said many times I was a long-distance telephone wife. Bob and I could never get together. When I was in a picture, he was on vacation. When I was off for a few weeks, he was sent to someplace halfway around the world. The best we could do, usually, was shake hands at the door as we came in and out."

Louella Parsons wrote in her column: "It is almost certain that the Italian girl had nothing to do with the Taylors' decision to part. Trouble started long before Bob went to Rome. I spoke to Barbara and I am inclined to think when they decided to end their marriage it came suddenly. It was Bob, however, who asked for his freedom."

On February 21, 1951, looking chic in a slim toast-colored suit with a matching hat topping her gray curls, Barbara Stanwyck told the court in a three-minute hearing (one of the shortest divorces on record) that her husband, Robert Taylor, was tired of being married and wanted to be a bachelor again.

"He said he had enjoyed his freedom during the months he was making a movie in Italy," she testified. "He wanted to be able to live his life without restrictions. I was very shocked and very grieved over it and was quite ill. For several weeks I was under the care of my physician."

Helen Ferguson was Barbara's witness and testified that she received an urgent and hysterical telephone call from her friend to come right over to the Taylor house. "When I got there, I found Barbara in a tragic emotional state. She said she was going to give Bob the freedom he wanted."

The judge said, "That will be enough. Divorce granted."

Barbara asked the court for permission to drop the surname Taylor and she was awarded their $100,000 mansion, all furnishings, and fifteen percent of Taylor's earnings until she remarried or either party died.

As she left court, Barbara refused comment on rumors that her matinee idol husband wanted his freedom because he had fallen in love with an Italian beauty. "I don't know," she said with a crooked smile. "You'll have to ask Mr. Taylor about that!"

When she was asked if she had a new boyfriend, Barbara widened her eyes and shuddered. "Oh, no! I've had enough. I don't want any more of that!"

Although Barbara did not want to discuss Bob with

even her closest friends and absolutely refused to talk about him throughout the years to come, two decades later she commented: "Bob wanted it and I don't want someone if he doesn't want me. 'There is the door, you can open it. That's all you have to do. If you can't open it, I'll do it for you.' "

The divorce hearing in 1951 made headlines and the following day the shapely Italian bit player had a press conference in Rome, which was duly covered by the newspapers.

BOB'S "BIG LOVE" SEES NO HITCH IN HER PLANS

Rome: Redheaded Lia De Leo, for whose love Robert Taylor ostensibly broke up with Barbara Stanwyck, today was so little impressed with the "great lover" of American films that she indicated she would rather remain "good friends" with Taylor than marry him.

She admitted she was truly Bob's true love when he was in Rome, but she said marriage with Taylor did not seem to be in the cards, though "if it depended on him alone, I am sure we would marry." She said the breakup between the Taylors was inevitable. "I knew this would happen ever since he was here. He was tired of his wife and he told me so. It was evident that, after meeting me, a divorce was the only possible solution."

The divorced Lia said she was reluctant to marry again after having had one previous disheartening experience. "Yet I might yield to his persistence, though after my first marital experience I have become convinced it is better to be good friends than to be hampered by marriage ties. I think I shall be very good friends with Robert instead of being his wife."

Lia De Leo posed for photographers in a striped bathing suit, which showed every curve to its best advantage.

Taylor refused comment, but he was hounded by the

press. Once, while trying to have a quiet cocktail with
Rex Harrison, he blew up over persistent questions about
Lia. "What about her? I'm here, aren't I? Is she with me?"

Despite his sarcasm, reporters asked about his social
life.

"Well, what about it?" he scowled. "I've nothing to
hide! My life's an open book these days. In fact everybody's getting into the act. I've read so many different
things about myself that half the time even I can't keep up
with what I'm doing—or rather what I'm supposed to be
doing!"

He told Purvis that, despite the fact privacy in Hollywood was not possible, he would have to find a way to
prevent hurting Barbara anymore. If they could not reconcile, he would keep his personal life top secret to prove
to her he still cared. "As a matter of fact," he said, "I went
out with several girls in Rome, but I always took them to
small places outside the city. But Lia was always on the
set because she was an extra. Or around the hotel. No way
I could be discreet. I realize now she meant nothing more
than the others."

Barbara was so upset as a result of the divorce that she
moved out of their mansion immediately and auctioned
off most of the furniture. Among the six hundred items to
go on the block were sixty-five paintings, among them a
Renoir, and a series of ten studies of pioneer women by
Fredric Remington. Barbara's bed sold for $360, and
Taylor's laced leather headboard and end table built into
it, including a carved wood horse supporting a lamp, sold
for $630.

Two days after the auction, Barbara and Bob were seen
dining at Ciro's in Hollywood. Bubbling and sparkling,
she glowed when reporters approached. "There's no use
trying to keep it a secret," she sighed. "I'm carrying a
torch for Bob, but it is too early to say whether we will be
reconciled."

She confided that this was her second date with Taylor since the divorce decree, which would not become final for a year. He refused comment, as usual, but the ebullient Barbara was eager to express her feelings. "There will be no other man in my life." When Stanwyck said these words—words she would repeat for almost a lifetime—she was pathetically convincing to even the most persistent skeptic.

Taylor was sincerely trying to recapture what he and Barbara had when they were courting in the late thirties. He hoped that champagne, roses, romantic music, dancing, and frivolous conversation might bring them closer together and perhaps salvage a marriage. Bob did not want to be categorized as another handsome movie star getting a divorce. Neither he nor Barbara had ever "gone Hollywood" or given into the crazy lavish life-style so common in tinseltown. Nor did they take love and marriage lightly. Before the final chapter, Bob would be true to himself and "try like hell" to rekindle the flame. It was worth a try because he sincerely liked Barbara and respected her even more.

Barbara said she had only threatened Bob with divorce in Rome and to her amazement he took her up on it. She wanted to frighten him, to bring him to his senses, but had not for a moment contemplated divorce. Although she was not one to forgive and forget, Barbara did—"Just this once."

The press was very intrigued by the Taylor divorce testimony, Bob's affair, Barbara's tears, and then their reunion over a candlelit table. Typical of the comments which came fast and furious were:

"She always told Bob what to do and how to do it. Could anyone forget when she gave him a convertible? Why, she even showed him how to drive it!"

"Barbara and Bob could find nothing to do together in their spare time. If she had forced herself to suffer through a few more flights with him and tried to endure a camping trip and traveled to his side when he was on location, she might have held on to Bob."

"They simply got tired of each other and their way of life. Barbara was and always will be a dedicated actress and I think her career came first even though she will never love anyone else but Bob."

"Maybe they should have adopted children. Bob loves kids, but Barbara didn't have time for them. Dion was a sad example. She and Bob had only one thing in common—the movie industry."

Taylor's psychiatrist friend said, "Bob didn't want to lose Barbara because she represented his mother. In one sense he'd be lost without her as any boy is without maternal love and comfort. But a man does not marry his mother. Bob knew this and he was determined to change the mother image into the wife and lover image. It couldn't be, despite the romantic atmosphere and dedicated attempts. He would have to let go, but not without the proper love and respect any son wants from his mother. Bob had grown up. He wanted a wife, children, and a home. Leaving the nest wasn't easy, however."

Taylor began dating other women, but very discreetly, and stuck to his vow to Purvis to keep his personal life top secret and prevent Barbara from being hurt.

One of his favorite girlfriends was the honey blond actress, Virginia Grey. She had been Clark Gable's favorite for seven years and supposedly they would marry, but in a drunken state he eloped with Lady Ashley. Several days after Gable's sudden marriage, Taylor got in touch with Virginia.

He always arranged to meet her at her home in Encino bringing with him steaks, wine, and his favorite records. She assumed he did not want to be seen in public because his divorce was not yet final. "I just took this for granted," Virginia said, "because Bob never said anything about

Barbara. I know he enjoyed cooking steaks and relaxing at home. I suppose at that particular time he did not want to be seen with other women because Barbara was still in love with him and they were seeing each other. Everyone knew that.

"Bob was down-to-earth and wonderful company, but in many ways it was very strange. At the end of the evening he would manage to disappear without saying good night. The first time this happened I spent hours looking for him, thinking something had happened to him. Nothing of the sort. Bob had simply gone home. He did not want to go through that sticky phony 'I'll call you tomorrow or see you next week' business, so he left. Then he'd call and nothing was mentioned about his disappearance.

"He meant well. When he was on location making a film, he wrote to me regularly. Often Bob would say he was sorry I did not come along, but he never asked. Or he'd mention trying to call me, but I wasn't home. I was. I never talked about seeing Bob and there was never any mention of us in the gossip columns. Nor were there any rumors.

"How Barbara found out, I will never know, but I learned the hard way that she resented any woman he dated. Several years later—long after their divorce and his remarriage—I appeared in a movie with her, and the first day on the set she let me have it with words I cannot repeat. There was no mention of Bob, but she had no other reason to dislike me so intensely. I had done the unpardonable. I had gone out with Robert Taylor."

$\mathcal{B}$arbara Stanwyck had seen the last of her great movies, as a result, to a large degree, of the birth and popularity of television. Robert Taylor, however, became, during the fifties, the country's knight in shining armor in *Ivanhoe, Knights of the Round Table*, and *Quentin Durwood*. He fared better than most Hollywood stars in the fifties, due in large part to these films being big spectacles and the sort of entertainment TV couldn't provide, before terminating the longest running contract in movie history—twenty-five years with MGM.

Barbara accepted *The Man with a Cloak*, teaming up with Joseph Cotten. Jim Backus, also in the film, referred to this movie as a "pretentious piece of merde." Oblivious of a broken heart, Stanwyck was well prepared, and she was admired by her coworkers even more than usual because she did not allow her personal grief to interfere with her work.

Barbara was eager to make *Clash by Night* with Paul Douglas and Robert Ryan. In this rewrite of a Clifford Odets play, Stanwyck portrayed a dissatisfied fisherman's wife who has an affair with a crude cad. Marilyn Monroe, in one of her first important movie roles, was habitually late, nervous, unprepared, and clumsy. Robert Ryan remembered, "It upsets everyone's timing when someone like Marilyn doesn't show up on schedule and then stumbles and stammers. Missy and Paul and I were furious, ready to tell her exactly how we felt, but we melted. She was so childish—almost angelic and innocent. Marilyn never deliberately did anything wrong and we realized she was oblivious. Barbara said Marilyn was carefree and, even when Marilyn blew her lines again and again, Barbara was patient and understanding. I liked Barbara, but never thought of her as being quite so sympathetic. But she was and we all were."

Ryan mentioned that Marilyn was not the only reason there was tension while making *Clash by Night*. "The movie dealt with adultery and a marriage almost destroyed by a third party. Barbara had just suffered through this situation and some of the lines were not easy for her to say."

Fritz Lang, the director, also understood the delicate subject of the film, which closely resembled Stanwyck's recent plight. "One morning she came to me and complained about a particular scene because it was badly written," Lang said. "I knew the scene and thought it was well written. I asked her if I could speak frankly and she said, 'Naturally.' I told her I thought the scene reminded her of a rather recent event in her private life and that was the reason she thought it was badly written and couldn't play it. Barbara looked at me and said, 'You son of a bitch!' turned around and did the scene. We only had to shoot it once."

With great depth and understanding Barbara spoke these lines, "People change. You find out what's important and what isn't. What you really want." She won the Motion Picture Exhibitors Laurel Award for her seething performance in *Clash by Night*.

Clash by Night was a struggle for Barbara not solely because of Marilyn's amateurishness or the film's subject matter; her health was poor and her resistance lowered. Toward the completion of the film she was ill, but forged ahead without telling anyone. The day after the final scene was shot, Barbara was rushed by ambulance to the hospital with pneumonia. During her brief recovery she accepted the lead in *Jeopardy* with Barry Sullivan, but she was more interested in beginning *Titanic* with Clifton Webb and a very young Robert Wagner, whom Barbara took under her wing as she had William Holden in *Golden Boy.*

But Robert Wagner fell in love with Barbara Stanwyck. Though only in his twenties, he told a friend it didn't matter that she was approaching fifty. They were inseparable during the filming. Just as Taylor had been sixteen years earlier, Wagner was in awe of the self-made "movie queen" who once had been a penniless orphan and hoofer. He valued every word she said and watched her every move. He was eager to learn and she was willing to teach. This giant crush of Wagner's was indeed fate, coming so soon as it did after Stanwyck had lost Taylor. The coincidence of the first name Bob and the similar innocent youthfulness she had adored in Taylor also contributed to her interest, as did young Bob's determination to be more than just another handsome face in Hollywood. She let Wagner sit by her side, talk out his problems on the telephone, and take up as much of her time as he needed.

Wagner said, "She is a sensitive lady beneath that tough outer shell. She changed my whole approach to my work, made me want to learn the business completely. She started me thinking. It means a lot when someone takes time with a newcomer—especially Barbara Stanwyck."

Titanic did not feature Barbara in as many scenes as she was used to, but her role was dynamic and each time she appeared, it was a turning point in the story. Her final farewell to Clifton Webb as the ship is sinking is one of her better performances. During the filming of the story's tragic ending, Stanwyck admitted she felt the sorrow and impact of being in a lifeboat watching the great ship *Titanic* sinking to the tune of "Nearer My God to Thee": "The night we were filming the scene of the dying ship in the outdoor tank at Twentieth Century-Fox, it was bitter cold. I was forty-seven feet up in a lifeboat swinging on the davits. The water below was agitated into a heaving rolling mass and it was thick with other lifeboats full of women and children. I looked down and thought: if one of these ropes snaps now, it's good-bye for you. Then I looked up at the faces lining the rail, those left behind to die with the ship. I thought of the men and women who had been through this thing. We were re-creating an actual tragedy and I burst into tears. I shook with great racking sobs and couldn't stop."

Stanwyck won another Laurel from the Motion Picture Exhibitors for *Titanic*.

After the movie was finished, Robert Wagner continued to call on Barbara Stanwyck. They had dinner together occasionally and a few rumors floated around Hollywood. Barbara said it was all nonsense. "The picture of Bob and me in the paper was a laugh. Clifton Webb was dining with us, but they cut him out!" Wagner considered the gossip silly, but he was quoted as saying at the conclusion of *Titanic*, "Barbara is a great memory . . . great enjoyment and love."

Concerning her next opus, *All I Desire*, Stanwyck said, "I'm playing the type of part I've played many times—a bad woman trying to make up for past mistakes. But I like gutsy roles. Namby-pambies have no interest for me. I'd rather not act at all than do a Pollyanna. I've got to play human beings. I think I understand the motives of the bad women I play. My only problem is finding a way to play my fortieth fallen female in a different way from the thirty-ninth."

The *New York Times* panned *All I Desire.* Variety referred to it negatively as "tear-jerking and soap-operaish." But Stanwyck was given credit for doing her best.

Taylor gave Barbara a diamond heart for her forty-fourth birthday. Before his departure for Europe to make *Ivanhoe,* he dined with her. According to friends, he called her often when he was abroad. Both said they could not predict what the future would hold.

Bob's next film, *Above and Beyond,* teamed him with Eleanor Parker, the actress who complemented him the most. Apparently they affected each other the same way in private life. Parker was in the process of separating from her second husband and attracted to Bob—who returned her affections. They were seen lunching together in New York while on a promotion tour for *Above and Beyond.* Their "friendship," the press said, was "mutual admiration and professional devotion." Eleanor told reporters she would very much like to do another movie with Bob, but her relationship with him was platonic; to prove it, she took out pictures of her three children. The fact that she and Bob were seeing each other privately was a well-known fact, but generally unknown to the public.

Despite protestations to the reporters, they might have married, but Eleanor was in many ways like Barbara, although instead of being older than Taylor, she was eleven years younger. Friends say it is difficult to say why Eleanor and Bob did not reach the altar, but the consensus was that she was an independent woman and somewhat domineering—problems Bob had faced in his first marriage.

His only comment was, "She makes me nervous."

Nevertheless, they were in love, but Bob managed to carry on his other affairs so that none were aware that the others existed.

The only serious mention of an involvement with anyone was with Barbara. After the divorce they were seen
together more often than during their marriage. She was
eager to "try again," but their attempts failed even though
he desperately wanted her friendship. One reporter said,
"They always look happy together now, just like old
times. They never engage in serious conversation. Always
smiling and laughing. He was very attentive to her. We
asked them about a reconciliation knowing it would never
happen. Even though Miss Stanwyck was glowing, it was
not with hope."

Barbara continued her open friendship with Robert
Wagner, but was reportedly romantically involved with
French actor Jean-Pierre Aumont, whose wife, Maria
Montez, had died in 1951. Barbara was forthright: "Jean-
Pierre is a wonderful person, but there was never any ro-
mance. He hasn't gotten over the death of his wife whom
he loved very much."

Barbara was unhappy and lonely now. Her films were
bad, Bob was gradually pulling away from her and she
was having a showdown with her son, Dion, who had decided to drop out of school and join the army. The Korean
War was raging, and friends begged Barbara to meet the
twenty-year-old boy she had adopted two decades ago.
Regardless of her feelings, she might never forgive herself
if she did not.

Barbara met Dion for lunch. She greeted him with an
outstretched gloved hand and proceeded to tell him how
to conduct himself in the army. There were no kisses or
hugs. No warmth. Just a lecture and good luck. After five
years, Dion expected more from her. As of this writing
and to this author's knowledge, that was the last time
mother and son have seen or spoken with each other.

Dion spoke out to the press in later years blaming his
confusion on loneliness and everyone telling him to forget
that Barbara Stanwyck was his mother. Yet Dion still

feels guilty that he was not the child Barbara wanted. Hurting for love, he didn't know which way to turn, and that's when his real problems began.

The year 1953 was not a good year for Stanwyck. She portrayed yet another floozy, this time in *Blowing Wild*. Even with costars Gary Cooper and Anthony Quinn, the *New York Herald Tribune* was not impressed: "*Blowing Wild* is labeled cheap from the very beginning when it has some difficulty making up its mind whether it is imitating *High Noon* or *Treasure of Sierra Madre*. It soon lapses into its own brand of corny sensation in a story about strong men fighting bandits in the Mexican oil fields with Barbara Stanwyck climbing all over Gary Cooper in a dime-novel version of grand passion."

The *New York Times* labeled the film a "lost cause" accentuated by painful dialogue. Stanwyck: "Why do you always fight against me?" Cooper: "Because you're no good."

The Moonlighter with Fred MacMurray fared no better. The *New York Times* blasted it as "shapeless, dull, and a low-budget affair." The *Times* concluded that both Stanwyck and MacMurray had picked themselves a "sow's ear."

In *The Moonlighter* Barbara finally got to do her own stunts for the first time in a while. One was sliding down a waterfall into a fast-moving river and she hit every rock on the way down. Barbara was brusied and hurt but said nothing.

Besides her disappointing movies, the year 1953 was depressing for Barbara in other ways—a dramatic turning point in her life and the beginning of heartaches she did not imagine possible. She could do nothing to reverse the downhill trend of her career. The desire and ability to work hard were just as strong, but Stanwyck's destiny was no longer in her control. Money would never be a problem again ("She practically owns A & P," a friend

said), but with her small fortunc she seemed able to ac-
quire only a comfortable house with her loyal maid, Harriett Coray. Retiring never entered Barbara's mind, and to
her a life of traveling and socializing was boring and
worthless. Still carrying that blazing torch for Bob
blocked her heart from other romantic intrusions. With
two heartbreaking marriages behind her, Barbara was no
fool. At forty-six, she looked for little other than brief innocent flings with younger men. Her closest friends, those
who adored her, claim she was attracted to the Taylor im-
mage: the boyish and immature nature combined with a
beautiful face and trim body. Her adversaries referred to
them as "studs."

Barbara was a hearty drinker and tried to drown much
of her loneliness and frustration with liquor. Again those
people in Hollywood who had little respect for the
woman Stanwyck said she drank far too much and often
to excess. Witnesses at parties thought she looked foolish
in her attempts to lure attractive men so openly. Shock
turned to pity when it became apparent Barbara spent
much of her time drinking at home alone.

She had a valid reason because Taylor was living with a
beautiful German actress named Ursula Thiess, a Howard Hughes discovery.

Ursula and Bob were introduced on a blind date by her
agent in April 1952. They were often seen at nightclubs
usually to bolster her career and lend her the image of an
up-and-coming Hollywood actress. As soon as they entered the social scene, they were no longer part of it. Ursula surprised Taylor one night by suggesting thcy dine
in her tiny apartment. She prepared German pancakes,
and from then on their evenings were spent at her home.

Living together was not socially accepted in 1953 any
more than it had been in 1939, but Hollywood insiders
didn't care who was living with whom. It was common
knowledge that Bob was sharing Ursula's apartment with

her. Bob was discreet, though, because he was still pro-
tecting Barbara and seeing her occasionally. He had not
completely given up hope for a reconciliation and had no
intention of marrying anyone else.

Taylor's formal address was his mother's home and as
far as anyone else was concerned, that was where he was
living. No one could prove otherwise.

Barbara was very careful with the press these days. She
told them: "Bob and I are getting along just fine. That is
important—to be good friends once again. It took a lot of
doing. I am tired of conjecture. Conjecture is the cheapest
thing in the world. Bob and I go to a nightclub or have
dinner and talk. I know what I know. Bob knows what he
knows. Other people don't."

With the beautiful Ursula on his arm, reporters clamored for Bob's engagement announcement. "I am definitely not betrothed," he insisted. "Of course I want to
get married again. I don't know when or to whom, but it
would be a dismal prospect to be a bachelor for the rest of
my life. Ursula is truly lovely. She has the most beautiful
eyes I've ever seen. They're brown with specks of gold.
And her lashes are at least a half inch long—I'm not exag-
gerating."

Ursula, however, was not going to wait for Bob to make
up his mind. When it became obvious he was not going to
marry her, she told him her young daughter was coming
from Germany to live with her, "and it wouldn't look
right having you in my apartment. We can meet in the afternoon, if you wish."

In a huff Taylor moved back with his mother until he
left for Egypt to film *Valley of the Kings* with his former
love, Eleanor Parker. His letters to Ursula were returned
unopened. When he got back to Hollywood, Bob called
Ursula immediately, but she refused to see him. On the
set of *Rogue Cop*, which he was making at the time, one
of the crew mentioned seeing Bob at a party with Barbara.

Taylor hissed, "I wasn't with her! I just dropped by for a few minutes and she happened to be there. That's all. Why doesn't everyone bug off!"

He jumped down a reporter's throat for asking him where the beautiful Ursula was these days. Taylor said he didn't know. There was some mention about her seeing other men. Bob repeated he didn't know and, furthermore, "I don't give a damn!" But he did, and it had never occurred to him Ursula might become interested in another man. A few weeks later he called her begging for a minute of her time. She said guests were coming for dinner. He insisted there was something she had to see. A few hours later Robert Taylor gave Ursula Thiess an engagement ring—and she accepted. He said they had no plans to marry, but three weeks later—on May 24, 1954—they eloped to Jackson, Wyoming.

Barbara sent a congratulatory telegram as soon as the announcement was made the following morning, but she was in deep shock. The threads of reconciliation she had clung to desperately were finally torn. His romances with Eleanor Parker and Ursula Thiess were passing phases, she thought. Hadn't she waited for him to get through the aches and pains of becoming a star? And the sting of fame and money mingled with the fickle public and the scorching press? Even his affair with Lana Turner? And those horrid years when he was accused of being gay? Then Lia De Leo? All of these phases passed, but she was still a part of his life. Eleanor Parker had been a threat, but somehow Barbara knew he would eventually leave her. Then came Ursula. Why should she be different from the others? Ursula had two children by a previous marriage. Could Bob handle this and would he want to? Probably he would not at the age of forty-three.

It had taken Bob a long time to buy the ring and he kept it to himself for several weeks before giving it to Ursula. Obviously he had doubts. During this time he saw Barbara, but not as regularly. In later years Taylor told Purvis that at the time of his marriage to Ursula he still felt some loyalty to Barbara. "It hurt me to hurt her," Bob said. "Regardless of how lonely I was and the fact I deserved a life of my own, it bothered me terribly to completely break the tie."

Purvis reminded Bob that he had to pay Barbara fifteen percent of his salary. Wasn't that enough?

"I thought she might waive that," Taylor sighed. "I honestly thought she'd do that much."

Barbara had no intention of doing so. He would pay her until the day he died.

Now, more than ever, Barbara wanted to work. She desperately needed to keep busy and put the past out of her mind for as many hours in the day as possible. "I'm an actress and an actress acts," she said.

But the only good script offered her was *Executive Suite* with a cast of great stars: June Allyson, Fredric March, Nina Foch, Walter Pidgeon, Paul Douglas, Shelley Winters, Dean Jagger, and Louis Calhern. But most important of all was William Holden. Barbara's part as the mistress of a dead tycoon was a small but effective one. She was eager to do it and especially happy to be reunited with her golden boy, Bill Holden.

Helen Rose, who designed the costumes, was horrified when she discovered that Barbara had worn one of her dresses backward. Stanwyck was devastated. She knew how expensive it would be to reshoot a day's work. But Helen said that when the rushes came back there was no need to reshoot—the dress looked great on Barbara backward!

Executive Suite was a fine film and Barbara won her third Laurel Award.

With George Sanders and Gary Merrill, Barbara appeared in *Witness to Murder*. In this cheap thriller she had an opportunity to release her emotions similar to the way she had in *Sorry, Wrong Number*, though the two films could not otherwise be compared in terms of quality.

If Barbara was disappointed to have her name on the marquee above *Witness to Murder*, she had no idea how bad things could get. The trend was downward and *Cattle Queen of Montana* pushed her even further into a slump.

"Dreadful! Awful!" she cringed. "You wonder how such a thing could happen. The answer is simply that I made a horrible mistake. One gets taken in by what seems like a good idea and a sort of rough, temporary screenplay, and you sign to do the picture without ever having seen a completed script.

"Within one week after the start of the shooting, everybody on the set knows that the thing is just not jelling. But by that time, you're hooked. So you do your best and you privately hope that nobody goes to see it."

Ronald Reagan, who suffered through this film with her, said, "We filmed in Montana. The lakes up there were only around forty degrees, but Barbara insisted on doing a swimming scene, instead of allowing her double, because a realistic closeup of her actual face would be more effective. She was in that icy water a long time and never complained. By now she was riding well, too, and did not use a stunt girl. Despite a bad script, this was good experience for her in the rugged outdoors which would prove rewarding in the future."

Important critics did not bother reviewing *Cattle Queen of Montana*, but Hollywood insiders did. One of them remarked on her professional dedication, "Barbara went camping with Bob once and said she would never do that again. She hated guns and was afraid of horses—both Taylor's passions. But when she had to, Barbara roughed it up in *Cattle Queen of Montana* like she was a country girl. She turned blue in the lake, crawled over logs, used a gun, and sat a horse well. One has to wonder why, if she loved Bob so much, she did not do these things with him. Not that Bob gives a damn, but it would be interesting to find out his thoughts on the matter. Ursula didn't know a damn about his hobbies, but she dived in and won the guy she loved. Barbara had no conception how to love. She's one in a million because her heart and soul belong to acting. They don't make them like her anymore."

The Blackfeet Indians in Montana thought so, too. They "adopted" Stanwyck and gave her the name Princess Many Victories III for her endurance in the many scenes she insisted on doing personally. In an impressive ceremony they made her a member of their Brave Dog Society. They said, "Princess Many Victories III. She rides. She shoots. She has bathed in waters from our glaciers. She has done very hard work—rare for a white woman. To be a member of our Brave Dog Society is to be known as one of our brave people. Princess Many Victories is one of us."

Another "forget-me-please" movie followed, *The Violent Men* with Edward G. Robinson and Glenn Ford. If Stanwyck was distressed about this film, she was almost ruined by *Escape to Burma* with Robert Ryan. The *New York Times* hooted, "Even the monkeys seem bewildered!" And in 1956 yet another loser, *There's Always Tomorrow* with Fred MacMurray and Joan Bennett.

With one dreadful script following on the heels of another, the middle fifties was a frustrating period for Barbara Stanwyck. She was still popular at the box office, but was losing out to Shirley Booth, Joan Crawford, Katharine Hepburn, Audrey Hepburn, Bette Davis, Grace Kelly, Susan Hayward, Deborah Kerr, Jennifer Jones, Ingrid Bergman, and Elizabeth Taylor.

But the worst blow to Barbara's pride was the birth of Taylor's first child, Terry, on June 18, 1955. She was on a set when an announcement about Bob's son was made on the loudspeaker. Tears swelled in her eyes as she tried to keep her true emotions under control, then she could bear it no longer and rushed to her dressing room. One of the cast said, "At first we thought Barbara was overjoyed, but when she left the set in such a state, it was obvious that she was devastated. Taylor's marriage was sealed. Barbara was unable to give Bob a child during their ten years together. We wondered if she shed tears of joy, tears of envy, tears of jealousy, or tears of frustration. When she came back to her chair on the set, Barbara was not herself. There were no smiles. We were all embarrassed because we had cheered at the news about the birth of Terry Taylor. But we were very, very happy for Bob. He waited a long time. As for Barbara that day, she did her best to make us feel comfortable around her, but it was impossible to cover up the loneliness on her face."

In typical Stanwyck fashion she forged ahead to try to find a quality movie. Columbia's *Pal Joey* with Frank Sinatra was expected to be a blockbuster and she wanted the role of the socialite who falls in love with Sinatra. It was a small role, but meaningful and explosive. Harry Cohn, even though he was partly responsible for discovering Barbara, felt she was not sensual enough and that the part had to reek of sexuality. When Cohn could not get Marlene Dietrich, he overlooked Stanwyck and chose Rita Hayworth.

The choice films were definitely not going to Barbara Stanwyck in the middle and late fifties. Hollywood was changing and, though she was willing to change with it, for years she was typecast as the tough dame or, more frequently, as the tough woman in Westerns such as Zane Grey's *The Maverick Queen* with Barry Sullivan and Scott Brady. It wasn't a good film, but Stanwyck worked just as hard as if her role were a potential Academy Award nomination. She knew everyone's lines and their exits and entrances, often prompting the others who forgot. She said she could understand how actors could lose interest when doing a bad film and put less into it, but she did not have the heart, professionalism, or pride to do that.

The major critics did not bother reviewing *The Maverick Queen* in 1956.

Barbara looked forward to costarring with James Cagney in *These Wilder Years* as the head of an adoption agency, a film she thought might give her popularity a boost. She was disappointed.

The *New York Times* said, "The intent of this little drama is lofty enough . . . and Mr. Cagney and Miss Stanwyck go at it with becoming restraint and goodwill. But the story is hackneyed and slushy and Roy Rowland's direction is so slow and pictorially uninteresting that the picture is mawkish and dull."

The *New York Daily News* agreed: "Although the veterans are incapable of inadequate performances, they are not at their best in this dramatization. A major handicap is the static presentation of a story already devitalized by excess padding."

Crime of Passion offered Stanwyck an excellent role as the bored wife of a detective (Sterling Hayden) who commits murder in order to get him a promotion. The story was good, and Stanwyck gave a superb performance as did Hayden, but this low-budget B-film was barely noticed.

After *Crime of Passion* in 1957 she was offered few scripts. Ten years before Stanwyck had many to chose from and she could not keep up with the good roles that came along. Taylor canceled his contract with MGM by mutual consent because he said he could not save money on a straight salary. But between his pension and tax-deferred monies, he parted after twenty-five years with almost a million dollars, which he immediately invested in Ursulor Rancho, the Taylors' rambling but cozy and simple house deep in Mandeville Canyon. The heavy wood coffee table in front of the ceiling-high fireplace was the only item he salvaged from the divorce. On the 110 acres of ground Taylor raised quarter horses.

Although Bob was starting to feel the effects of poor scripts like the other movie greats, with few exceptions his films were far superior to Barbara's. In 1953 Barbara had said, "As long as the customers want to see me, I'll continue to make movies. After all, they shoot old horses." And continue to make movies she did.

The team of Barbara Stanwyck and Joel McCrea was a good one in *Trooper Hook*. She portrayed the white prisoner of an Apache chief. With few lines in the first half of this film, Barbara's eyes and facial expressions were remarkable as she and her half-breed son return to society. Stanwyck and McCrea were well received by the critics, and the *New York Times* said, "But is anyone surprised?"

In 1957 Twentieth Century–Fox was preparing the script for *Woman with a Whip*. Marilyn Monroe begged the studio for the female lead, but Samuel Fuller who wrote the story and would produce and direct the film (later retitled *Forty Guns*) said he had Stanwyck in mind from the very beginning. As a whip-snapping outlaw, she was initially slated to be killed at the end, but the studio intervened for reasons unknown and she lives.

Amazingly she did a dangerous fall from a horse that a stuntman refused to do because it was too risky. Barbara took her chances, brushed herself off, and went along with the dialogue without missing a word.

Fuller said that, as far as he was concerned, Barbara Stanwyck was excellent as a queen, slut, or matriarch. Her class and appeal, he surmised, came from enormous sensitivity and "thousands of closeted thoughts she can select at will." Fuller hoped to star Barbara in a movie about Evita Perón, but never got around to it. He felt she would have been superb in this role.

When Stanwyck completed *Forty Guns*, she was fifty

and a veteran of eighty-one films. "My work is responsible for all the good things that have come into my life," she has said many times. "I feel most completely alive when I'm starting a new picture."

But she would not do that for a long time.

After working for thirty years making motion pictures, Barbara found herself without a script to read and none forthcoming.

"When people ask me why I'm not working," she exclaimed, "I tell them that no one has asked me! There are no parts for women my age because America is now a country of youth. Something is gone. They were beautiful, romantic films, not as realistic as today's, and I loved doing and watching them. Now we've matured and moved on. The past belongs to the past. But don't get me wrong. Just because I'm fifty doesn't mean I'm dead or in a wheelchair. I go with these new trends and enjoy and respect them for their own values."

Eight

L oretta Young was the first movie actress to appear on television with her own half-hour weekly show. Although she starred in only half of the episodes, all of them were introduced with the opening of a door and her spectacular entrance in a lavish full-length gown that swirled into the screen preceding a glamorous closeup. American women watched her show faithfully if for no other reason than to see the beautiful gown chosen for Loretta's grand entrance. She usually convinced them to stay tuned in, whether she was starring in the drama or not. At the end of her show she again appeared and tantalizingly asked, "See you next week?"

The word associated with Loretta Young's show was "class." There were few actresses who could do it quite as elegantly—unless it was Barbara Stanwyck.

She had made a guest appearance on Jack Benny's program, substituted on two occasions for Loretta Young when she was ill, and made four appearances on Dick Powell's "Zane Grey Theater" (similar in format to Loretta's show). She was eager to do her own television series, but did not want to be a carbon copy of Loretta. The networks disagreed, but were interested in her ideas. Barbara wanted to do a Western series, but the network brass were appalled. Miss Barbara Stanwyck sitting on a horse? Absolutely not! they gasped. There were too many Westerns anyway.

In a 1958 interview she said, "Of course I like TV. I'd be right in there now except that the brain boys (her agents) can't make up their minds what I should do. I want a Western series. But the brain boys said no. Westerns are on their way out.

"Way out! Not around my house they're not!" she said. "From six on it sounds like the last frontier around there. On Monday it's "Restless Gun" and "Wells Fargo." Tuesday it's "Cheyenne," "Sugarfoot," and "Wyatt Earp"—and so forth. Don't I ever get tired? Hell, no. I love it! I don't care what anybody says, I have a ball!"

When her agents rejected her idea based on James D. Horan's book *Desperate Women*, about courageous women on the western frontier, she fired them and hired another who was more receptive to her proposal.

"The title of Horan's book is a misnomer," she explained. "The women weren't desperate at all. They were just real. Some were good and some were bad. In all the Westerns these days—and as I said I love them—the women are always left behind with the kids and the cows while the men do the fighting.

"Nuts to the kids and the cows! There were women who went out and fought, too. That's what I want to do. People say it's not feminine. It isn't! Sure those women wore guns and britches. But don't kid yourself. They were all female!"

Stanwyck would have to wait seven years for her dream to come true. NBC-TV gave her a firm offer to do her own series, but not a Western. They felt she should follow Loretta Young's format. Barbara commented, "I'm too old and too wealthy to swallow that stuff!" And she repeated, "I want to play a real frontier woman, not one of those crinoline-covered things you see in most Westerns. I'm with the boys. I want to go where the boys go."

The negotiations continued for several years. Except for her few appearances on television, Barbara Stanwyck had not been working. When asked if she was finished as a film star, she said, "Sure, why not admit it? I couldn't stay up there forever. It's a man's world and it's getting worse. They aren't writing beautiful adult stories anymore. In the past three years I haven't been sent any scripts period! Oh, I know stars who say they can't find anything they want to do in films, but I wouldn't lie like that. I just haven't had any offers!"

NBC finally tried to pin her down about "The Barbara Stanwyck Theater," a series of half-hour episodes every week, but she insisted on complete approval of all scripts beforehand. At first NBC refused, but when they realized she had given up her fight for a Western, they agreed to her demand.

Stanwyck was not as glamorous and wasn't received as well as Loretta Young. Perhaps if she had preceded Loretta, it might have been different, but the timing was all wrong, and she was perceived as an imitation Loretta. "Besides," she said, "I was not the type to go swooping in and out of an elegant drawing room in those flourishing gowns. That wasn't me and I knew it."

A stranger to television techniques, just as she had been on a movie set fresh from the Broadway stage, Barbara followed the instructions of NBC directors. During the introduction to her weekly program she stood still, making her delivery dull and listless. Another drawback was her having to plug the sponsor, always awkward for stars. But, Barbara said, "the worst was being forced to read my lines from a teleprompter. I couldn't learn them because we didn't know the star or the story for the following week. Sometimes we were five or six weeks behind in the introductions. Sometimes the story hadn't been written, so we had to do six or seven at a time and often they had to be done over and over again."

"The Barbara Stanwyck Theater" was shown on Monday nights at ten. In an interview she told the press, "We are prepared to pay top price for our scripts. The foundation of a good show is the story, not the star. We have found some potential stories for our series and I hope I don't louse them up because they don't write stories for female stars anymore: the Crawfords, the Dunnes, and the Colberts. I don't know why motion pictures have great roles for men these days, but I'd like to present some meaty roles for women."

When reporters asked Barbara about Joan Crawford's statement that any movie star who appears on the boob tube is a traitor, Stanwyck sighed, "For me the reason is simple. I wasn't working in the movies and I wanted to work. What else is there for me to do? I have no hobbies. I suppose that makes me an idiot, but there it is. You're supposed to paint or sculpt or something. I don't. I like to travel, but a woman can't travel alone. It's a bore. And it's a darned lonesome bore. People say it's very nice that I'm going on television. How nice remains to be seen."

"The Barbara Stanwyck Theater" received mildly positive reviews, but was canceled after the first season. Despite this, she won the Emmy.

Having won the most prestigious award in the television industry, Barbara was shocked and terribly disappointed that her show was off the air. "I don't know who 'they' are, but they've decreed no more women on television. The only woman who will be left next year is Donna Reed. The rest of us have been dropped: Loretta Young, June Allyson, Dinah Shore, Ann Sothern, and me. And we all had good ratings. As I understand it, 'they' want action shows and have a theory that women can't do action. The fact is I'm the best action actress in the world. I can

do horse drags and jump off buildings and I have the scars
to prove it."

Meanwhile, ex-hubby Robert Taylor's show "The De-
tectives" ran on television for three years from 1959
through 1962. Columnist Hy Gardner asked Bob how he
liked seeing himself on television.

"I don't know," Bob said. "I don't own a TV set."

"What made you succumb to television?" Gardner
asked.

"M-O-N-E-Y."

Taylor's television series was very successful, but his
biggest thrill was his new baby daughter, Tessa, born on
August 16, 1959.

In 1961, after a four-year absence, Barbara was back
working in motion pictures with Laurence Harvey, Jane
Fonda, and Anne Baxter in *Walk on the Wild Side*, a fine
film bordering on the scandalous. Barbara was excellent
and many of her fans were delighted to see her back in
form. She enjoyed filming *Walk on the Wild Side*, but
working with Laurence Harvey brought out her fury
when he came on the set late. Her coworkers reported
that Barbara's vocabulary of four-letter words was prodi-
gious.

As for Harvey, he was quoted as saying, "I never could
quite decide which side of the camera she was working
on!"

Stanwyck said her role as madam of a New Orleans
bordello was a first. Cruel but warm and mysterious, her
character today would be spelled out: lesbian, in love with
one of her girls played by Capucine.

Barbara was satisfied with *Walk on the Wild Side*, but
the critics were disappointed. It was not a typical Stanwyck film and some of her old fans were unenthusiastic.
Because the theme of lesbianism was there but not ac-
knowledged. Stanwyck came off as the one who wasn't
sure what she was.

Immediately Stanwyck returned to television in episodes of "Rawhide," "The Untouchables," and "Wagon Train."

In 1963 she was given an award by the Professional Photographers of California who named her the First Lady of the Camera. "I guess they just got to the S's. I never know how I got it," she laughed.

A close friend said, "Barbara would always be shocked if she won anything for several reasons. The Oscar, for one. Her disappointment over being nominated so often and not winning was difficult to forget. She just never expected to win anything after those defeats. And she was the kind of actress who did not think of awards. She always did her best. Recognition to Stanwyck was admiration from the critics and her peers in Hollywood. When she did win an award, I can say that Barbara was one actress who was more surprised to receive it than anyone else."

The fifties had been terrible for Stanwyck; her life, both private and professional, gradually worsened. Many of the great motion picture studios closed their doors. Famous stars could no longer be seen coming and going through the tall prestigious gates every morning and afternoon in their custom-built limousines. The obituaries listed the names of great producers, directors, and moguls of the movie business.

The survivors were busy commuting by plane to New York for TV appearances, summer stock, or a Broadway play.

Stanwyck would always be a survivor, but, as strong as she was, there was one debilitating fear that severely limited her: her terror of planes. Thus she worked exclusively in the Los Angeles vicinity, and she never owned an apartment or house other than her permanent home near the studios.

Hollywood's Golden Era was over and the remaining strings broken. It was a depressing and frightening realization even for a gutsy hoofer from the tough streets of Brooklyn.

Stanwyck's life was unrewarding and unfulfilled.

This spunky orphan who took off her dancing shoes almost four decades ago had lost her confidence to face a live audience. She said that because of fear it would be impossible to return to the legitimate theater.

Everything she loved was disappearing around her—everyone, including Buck Mack, referred to as Uncle Buck, who had known Barbara as Ruby Stevens. It was Buck Mack who looked after her ranch when Taylor was courting her and who moved in with her and Bob after they were married. Mack was Barbara's only link to Dion Fay. Uncle Buck was devoted to both mother and adopted son throughout those bitter years.

Barbara cared for Mack when his health began to fail and, when this was no longer possible, she put him in the Motion Picture Country House and Hospital. In 1959 Buck Mack died and left a lonely void in Barbara's life. She arranged his funeral and felt that treasured memories were being buried with her dearest friend.

In 1961 Frank Fay died from a ruptured abdominal aorta. His estate of $200,000 was willed to Dion, but Barbara had no comment.

Barbara's living past was disappearing with those who shared her memories. Helen Ferguson remained close until, confined to a wheelchair, she settled in Palm Springs. Nancy Sinatra, Sr., remains Barbara's dearest and most trusted friend.

Her black maid, Harriett Coray, was a faithful companion who lived, worked, and traveled with Barbara for many years. They were devoted to each other, and Barbara would not allow segregation to separate her and Harriett when on location to make a film, prominent hotels did not permit blacks beyond the lobby. Barbara did not get angry or upset; rather she told the management to make a reservation for her, too, at the "other hotel downtown." Barbara and Harriett were then ushered to their posh suite.

Aside from a few other women friends, Stanwyck kept to herself. There were no men in her life. She attended the Oscar and Emmy awards with friends or alone. She detested formal affairs or cocktail parties; the nightclub days were over. Her favorite evenings were spent at house parties given by Nancy Sinatra, Sr. Every July 16 Nancy gave a "surprise" birthday party for her friend, but once Barbara failed to show up, calling the next day in tears because she hadn't been invited. According to the usual guests, she never was: it was accepted as a traditional event. One friend said it would appear that Barbara must have wanted special attention or sympathy, since no one else had misunderstood.

Like so many stars, Stanwyck drank quietly within the solitude of her home. Hollywood insiders generally did not discuss it because she was bothering no one, but failing to appear at her own party brought remarks such as, "Oh, Barbara had too much to drink and forgot about it," or "She probably had a few too many and decided to pass." If she was protected by those who both loved and hated her, it was simply a case of loyalty to the Hollywood code. After all, getting work was difficult and there was always the possibility of working with Stanwyck. Everyone was desperate and worried as television took over the industry.

There was also a great deal of sympathy for Stanwyck since she had no relatives. The loss of Buck Mack and the raunchy headlines about Dion were hurts anyone could understand. Her attempts to do a gracious television program had failed and it wasn't her fault.

A veteran Hollywood producer said, "So Barbara Stanwyck eased her pain with some booze. So what! What she does at home is her goddamn business. When that gal reports for work, she's always early, knows her lines and everyone else's. In fact, she knows better than I how to produce and direct. I don't know her personally, but when you work with such a dedicated actress, you feel as if you do. I have no quarrel with her. Naturally it's public knowledge the tragedies she's had. Some were her fault and more were not, but she suffered. Now she's entitled to do as she damn pleases and, if it's a few drinks alone in front of TV, God bless her. If I saw her fall on her face, for sure she would show up for work better prepared than any other actress or actor in Hollywood!"

If moviegoers considered Barbara Stanwyck an old-fashioned has-been, she fooled everyone by costarring with Elvis Presley in *Roustabout*. They were an unlikely couple, of course, and the idea was considered just publicity at first until producer Hal Wallis began filming and the public was mesmerized. But why film with Elvis? "Why?" she said. "Because I want to be exposed to the younger generation who probably never heard of me. Actually I had never seen an Elvis Presley movie. But I had worked for his producer, Hal Wallis, many times. When he called and said he had a part in a picture and mentioned Elvis Presley, I wondered what on earth I would do in a Presley film. I can't sing. I can't dance."

She explained her role. "I was the owner of a broken-down carnival and so on. Well, I liked the part, and the idea of working with Mr. Presley intrigued me. And I thought it would be fun. He was a wonderful person to work with. He asked for nothing.

"So many people expect the other—the swelled head and all that. So did I, frankly. But it was not the case. Elvis was a fine person. His manners are impeccable, he is on time, he knows his lines."

The *New York Times* gave *Roustabout* a good review: "It has three assets. One is Mr. Presley, perfectly cast and perfectly at ease as a knockabout, leathery young derelict who links up with a small-time transient midway. It also has, as the carnival owner, Miss Stanwyck, and where on earth have you been? And while the carnival canvas yields little in the way of dramatic substance, it does cue in eleven songs."

Although this was an exciting rebirth for Barbara, she was saddened once again, this time by the death of her brother Byron in 1964. He had been active as an extra in films, thanks to his sister, and on his own ability became the director of the Screen Extras Guild. Byron was filming a television commercial when he had a fatal heart attack.

Anxious to keep going despite the odds, Stanwyck tried again for a television series. The pilot for "The Seekers," about the FBI's Missing Persons Bureau, fell through. She was disappointed but did not give in. "I'm not giving up," she stressed. "I would go mad if I retired. I'm ready to work anytime. I'll take any part that comes along. I don't care about the money or the size of the role. All I care about is working."

She laughed about the rumors that she preferred being alone and living with her memories—she was even still identified with Robert Taylor, even though they had broken up fifteen years earlier. "How long am I supposed to carry that damn torch?" she complained. "I've heard what some people are saying—that I lock myself up in my house, pining away for him, and have no desire to do anything. Wrong. I'm sure no one wants to live alone, but you have to adjust."

In 1964 there was a strange turn of events indeed. Producer-director William Castle called Barbara about filming *The Night Walker*. She read the script and said she would love to do it. Castle wanted to know what she thought if Robert Taylor played the part of her attorney in the movie. "Well, I think it's wonderful," she said. "But you'd better ask Mr. Taylor how he feels about it."

No one consulted Taylor. He was out of town. Knowing how scarce good scripts were, his agent made a commitment that was almost impossible to dissolve. When Taylor returned to Los Angeles and found out he had been signed to *The Night Walker* opposite his former wife, he was livid. Trying to compose himself, he asked to see the script and added, "I'd like to give this some thought. It's rather startling. I wasn't prepared for this."

Taylor was upset for several reasons. He did not appreciate his agent's accepting anything without his consent. He did not want to work in a film with Barbara, despite the fact they had few scenes together in the movie. He certainly did not want to be forced to be "chummy" with her. And he was still paying her fifteen percent of his income: "That burns the hell out of me!"

It was too late for him to back out. Castle had notified the press, so by the time Bob read the script, complained to his agents, and fumed for several days, the news had been released about Barbara Stanwyck and Robert Taylor appearing in *The Night Walker* together.

"I might have gotten out of it," Bob said, "If I wanted to. But the money was worth it and those were the lean years in Hollywood when decent scripts were hard to find."

Reporters wanted to know how he felt about costarring with his ex-wife. "Who could pass up the opportunity of working with such a wonderfully talented woman?" he said politely.

After working with Barbara, he commented, "It doesn't seem possible I was ever married to her." Ursula was on the set with him and wanted to make friends with Barbara. Taylor was amusing and warm on the set, but when he and Ursula arrived home, he emphasized to his wife that he wanted nothing to do with Barbara socially. Ursula expressed pity for her. "She's lost most of her friends and has no family."

Taylor said he did not want Barbara in his home. Ursula knew when to back off, but she would bring it up again later, hoping he might change his mind.

The Night Walker was a suspense thriller. Stanwyck appeared in the majority of scenes as a wealthy woman who confused dreams with reality. Taylor, as her attorney, has a minor role but in the end is the surprise villain. He does little other than appear cool in a black pinstripe suit to calm his hysterical client. Castle's timing in *The Night Walker* was excellent. Stanwyck, plagued by insanity and stalked by a murderer, does a good job creating suspense to the highest pitch. Then Taylor appears just when one almost forgets he's in the film.

Many glamorous stars attended the premiere of *The Night Walker* and the lavish party afterward. Barbara and Bob were photographed together, often laughing, but never touching. These candid pictures would indicate that everyone was having a good time. The reviews were just as good: "William Castle has two old pros enriching the quality of his new eerie suspense thriller, *The Night Walker*. Barbara Stanwyck and Robert Taylor, coming out of semiretirement from films, are the invaluable assets in this Universal release."

Taylor said he didn't know he was in semiretirement and Barbara felt the same way. She went on a promotional tour with William Castle for *The Night Walker*, an unusual move for Stanwyck; she explained, "I own a percentage of this picture along with Bob and Mr. Castle. I hope it does well at the box office."

Ursula Taylor enjoyed seeing Bob in the limelight again and, though he had resisted costarring with Stanwyck, it was a successful venture. "We must have Barbara over for dinner soon," Ursula suggested casually.

"I don't think so," Bob said quietly.

"Why?" his wife asked.

"Because you don't know Barbara like I do."

Ursula never brought up the subject again.

Barbara just couldn't care. She was coming out of a

ten-year slump and loving every minute of it. Her next
undertaking was a television commercial, but it took a lot
of convincing and a lot of money among other entice-
ments, to get her to agree to it.

"A coffee commercial?" she screamed. "What on earth
for?"

Her agent laughed. "Sponsors care more about a
ninety-second commercial and want to pay you more than
any guest star gets for a ninety minute show! If you don't
do it, somebody else will jump at the chance. Why let
someone else laugh all the way to the bank?"

Barbara was still reluctant until the sponsor offered to
remodel her kitchen for nothing. She said her kitchen was
spotless, but, "Don't ask me why—that did it!"

Still in the whirlwind of getting back to work with
none other than Elvis Presley and then, suprisingly, Robert Taylor, Barbara felt alive again. But she had no idea
that her greatest dream was coming true—a television
Western.

Stanwyck did not immediately jump when ABC-TV
agreed that she should play Victoria Barkley in "The Big
Valley." As excited as she was, the big question for Barbara was, "Just what kind of a dame is the widow Barkley?" She refused to sign until her character was
established. "I do not want to play someone who tiptoes
down the staircase in crinoline and wants to know where
the cattle went. This is not me!"

Victoria Barkley, therefore, was a stunning woman
with class, wit, patience, and guts who rode a horse like
the wind and handled her buggy like a lady. She could
handle a gun as well as she poured tea. Victoria wore
britches and she wore velvet.

Cast as the four Barkley boys were Richard Long as
Jarrod, Peter Breck as Nick, and Lee Majors as the illegiti-
mate son, Heath, and Charles Briles as Eugene. Linda
Evans played Audra, the only Barkley daughter.

Both Lee Majors and Linda Evans were inexperienced

in 1965. Barbara was pleased, however, because she enjoyed helping eager young people in show business. She showed them the same attention that William Holden and Robert Wagner had received. Her encouragement meant a great deal to Evans and Majors, both of whom claim it was Stanwyck who taught them how to be professionals. Evans said that Barbara was someone who practiced what she preached. "We are like sisters to this day."

Stanwyck said Victoria Barkley was an old broad who combines elegance with guts. Thrilled with the role and determined to make "The Big Valley" a success, she ignored the bad reviews in the beginning. "By the time the bad review appears in print, the viewer has seen the show already. And he's just as liable to be defensive about a rap, figuring, 'That show wasn't as bad as all that!' In the end it is the viewers themselves who decide whether a show is a hit or not. They don't need any help to make up their minds. Bad reviews don't hurt me at all."

The reviews, however, did not please Barbara when they compared "The Big Valley" to "Bonanza" and Victoria Barkley to Ben Cartwright. "Our family is much stronger!" she insisted. "My sons are strong. They are real men. This is not one of those Mother-knows-best things! Hell, I wouldn't play one. Our family behaves like any normal family. We fight, argue, discuss things. We're not like some of the TV families today. I don't know where the hell these people are. I never see any of these people in real life. The woman I'm playing has plenty of battles with her boys. She's a very vital person. So are her sons. They have minds of their own."

Contrary to the critics' predictions—and supporting Barbara's assertion that quality will out—"The Big Valley" ran for four years in 112 episodes. Barbara appeared in all but seven and, if she thought making movies was hard work, she faced her toughest schedule yet. Studio shootings called for her to get up at four thirty every morning, and she was lucky to get home by seven thirty in the evening. On location Barbara was up at three thirty and not finished until nine thirty at night. Her whole life was "The Big Valley," and on weekends she studied her scripts to be always ahead of schedule.

"We do twenty-six shows in twenty-six weeks," she said, "and no one bothers to count the hours. In a television series such as ours, we are making twenty-six very fast movies. The script is there, the cameras are there, and you are there."

Stanwyck proved her skills once again by doing her own stunts. She was dragged by a horse 150 feet over rocks, fell off a horse, and was knocked cold when she was hit on the head by a rock. A hair piece had fortunately prevented serious injury.

Through all the bruises, late hours, and bad reviews, Stanwyck showed anger only when the rumor persisted that her show was ABC's version of NBC's "Bonanza." "I guess you have to be compared to something," she hissed, "so why not 'Bonanza?' Lorne Greene is the Loretta Young of the West. That's not for me!"

Barbara had gone a little too far this time. "Bonanza" was the number-one television show in the country, and many viewers were upset. Later she clarified: "I have been quoted as saying that I thought Lorne Greene was the Loretta Young of Western soap operas. I think I have been misquoted. What I did mean was that I felt he was too pontifical. When he passes judgment—that's that! When Lorne Greene has an opinion, it has to be right. Well, damn it all, I've had my own ranches. I am a horse-woman. I ran ranches and herds and bred livestock years before Lorne Greene even knew what a saddle looked like. And you don't run ranches anywhere by being pontifical about any bit of it. Nobody on any ranch can ever tell what's going to happen next. You can't afford to be too opinionated or too conceited. If you do, you portray the

West badly, and you do the West an injustice. The West was tough, hell-country, full of fights and wrongs and hardness. Pontifical wiseacres did not survive long out there."

Stanwyck kept her eye on "Bonanza" and continued to speak freely. When Dan Blocker, Hoss on the NBC series, complained about his salary, Barbara hit the roof. "What so-called artist is this who feels he is wasting his talent for $10,000 a week? He seems to feel the public loves him for himself as an actor. But what was he before playing Hoss? The love the public has given him is due to the role, the script, the actions of the person he is employed to play. If he is now a multimillionaire, as he says he is, what a shame he should continue to fool the public and to accept the love they give him."

She went on to say that actors are servants of the public. Money and fame are secondary to the true artist. "And to use terms like 'selling one's self,' isn't that an insult to the public that watches and likes a show and pays for it all? I probably won't be able to look at Blocker again, not in any role he plays. I'll probably feel he's just prostituting himself again in playing the next role—any role. But it is a fact that the public loves Hoss and has made Dan Blocker a rich man. It is like spitting at an audience that's standing and applauding. That's how I feel."

In 1966 Barbara won an Emmy for "The Big Valley" and was nominated again in 1967 and 1968. *Photoplay* magazine gave her their Editors Award, engraved "To the Eternal Star whose glamour, talent, and professionalism both on and off the screen have thrilled millions of fans throughout the years," and its readers voted her the most popular female star. *TV-Radio Mirror*'s Television Critics Poll was unanimous in naming Barbara Stanwyck as the best dramatic actress in television.

But it was the Screen Actors Guild Award she cherished the most. She was asked to present the award to

California's governor Ronald Reagan. Waiting backstage for her cue, Barbara became confused when she heard his voice on stage.

"The Screen Actors Guild Award is not presented just for longtime excellence onscreen," Reagan began. "It should be called, perhaps, an above-and-beyond award, because it is given for outstanding achievement in fostering the finest ideals of the acting profession.

"The individual to be honored has given of herself in unpublished works of charity and good citizenship. . . . So for performance of our craft, as well as for performance as a citizen, this award is being presented from actors to an actor, and I am very proud to present someone whom so many of us have worked with. We have known her in this profession as truly a professional and an exponent of our art and craft of the best. Barbara Stanwyck."

Trembling in the wings, she listened with disbelief. Obviously shaken and somewhat confused, she approached Reagan. Trying to compose herself, the tears came anyway, but her eyes were glistening with joy and gratitude. "I am very very proud at this moment. I love our profession very much. I love our people in it. I always have and I always will. And whatever little contribution I can make to the profession, or to anything, for that matter, I am very proud to do so. It is a long road. There are a lot of bumps and rocks in it, but this kind of evens it all out, when an event like this happens in your life. From a very proud and grateful heart, thank you very much."

Reagan explained to the press afterward, "Those who knew Barbara were concerned that if she suspected she was getting an award she wouldn't be there, so they invited her to come down and present the award to me. She was standing offstage, fully expecting to come out and make the presentation of the award to me, when she heard me making the presentation to her!"

One of the technicians who was standing near Stanwyck when she realized the award was going to be given to her, said, "I thought she would be sick. She was wearing gloves, I remember, and when the governor mentioned her name, she covered her face. It was as if she was glued to the floor. Someone had to take her arm and lead the way, and I wasn't sure she was going to make it. It was a mean trick, but as the governor said, she probably wouldn't have shown up."

In 1969 "The Big Valley" television series was canceled.

Barbara was disappointed and hurt, not only because a job came to an end but this time her costars had been like family and the set of "The Big Valley" her home away from home.

Although the cancellation of "The Big Valley" was a crushing blow, Barbara would face another blow more devastating in the year 1969.

Nine

*I*n August 1968 Robert Taylor fell to his knees from a violent coughing spell. He and Ursula had just returned from a house party at Rhonda Fleming's. After a cup of coffee and several aspirins, he retired, but Ursula insisted he make an appointment to see a doctor.

Waiting for the results of the X-rays, Bob told Tom Purvis, "I'm sorry I agreed to the tests. Couple of years ago the same thing happened. I've had a spot on my lung since I was a kid, and the damn doctors scared me six-feet-under until they told me I was fine. I swore I'd never go through that again. A few weeks ago I was a pallbearer at Dennis O'Keefe's funeral. He suffered a slow death from lung cancer after the surgeons cut him up. I don't know why a guy can't just die with some kinda respect, but the doctors—well, they don't letcha.

"They suspect pneumonia, but, Jesus, if I have lung cancer, no way can I keep it from the producers of 'Death Valley Days.' They won't wait to find out if I'm gonna make it or not. They'll have to replace me and I can't afford it. Far as I'm concerned, if they wanna cut, I might as well start diggin'. They're gonna getcha—not that they want to—they're just gonna getcha."

Taylor had been doing one movie a year as well as hosting and starring in "Death Valley Days" after Ronald Reagan left the show to run for governor of California.

Bob asked his ranch hand, Art Reeves, "Would you let them cut you up?" Art said he wouldn't. It was obvious to Ursula, Tom, and Art that Taylor had known his fate for some time. When his doctors confirmed a mass on the right lung, it was Ursula who begged Bob to undergo an operation. He wanted to think about it. She said: "If not for yourself, do it for the children and me."

He said his chances were better without going under the knife. "Once they're finished with me, I won't have much time left," he told her. "If I go about my business just the way I am, at least I'll be able to work."

But Ursula did not stop pleading with Bob and on October 8, a portion of his right lung was removed. An announcement was made to the press that Taylor had Rocky Mountain spotted fever, and the doctors assured Bob that was all it was. He was discharged, but Ursula took him home knowing he had cancer. In November Bob was sent back to the hospital for cobalt treatments. Cancer was not mentioned, but Bob knew he had it. Two operations followed the major one, and on December 3, 1968, the newspapers announced the truth.

He said it was the "one John Wayne role nobody wants. It was a tremendous shock of course. When I first went into surgery, I didn't know, but they found tumors in the right lung and that was it. But I've got to face it, I'm putting myself and all my faith in the hands of my doctors."

Several weeks after this interview he was admitted to Saint John's and reported in serious condition. On Christmas Day, the doctor told Ursula there was no hope: Bob had terminal cancer.

Taylor survived emergency treatment and returned to Ursulor Rancho in January knowing he did not have long to live.

Hollywood, loyal to the code, was faithful to one of the few legends left. John Wayne kept in touch and told Bob, "When they told me I had lung cancer, it was like being belted across the gut with a baseball bat, but I licked it!"

Dale Robertson, Chad Everett, Bob Stack, and Ronald Reagan were regular visitors. Barbara Stanwyck, heavily sedated and weak, came to see Bob several times.

Art Reeves, who knew his boss was running out of cash rapidly, was not overly anxious to see the wealthy actress on Taylor property. Reeves lived in a small apartment attached to "the barn" near the entrance to Ursulor Rancho. He was a big man who thought nothing of walking in front of an oncoming car to find out who was trespassing on the dirt road to the main house. He was not only close to Taylor but also the whole family: he was referred to as Uncle Art by Terry and Tessa. During these dark, depressing days, he was very protective of Taylor and resented Barbara's visits. At first he thought she was drunk and watched her carefully until he concluded she was drugged. He said he was always uneasy until she left.

"I knew it was a strain on Bob," Reeves said. "We were all trying to do things that were uplifting. The producers of "Death Valley Days" came over and insisted Bob go over some scripts and, when he wanted to be released from his contract, they refused. Anyone who talked to him acted as if everything was going to be all right. Barbara was the only one who didn't belong there. Maybe she was emotionally upset and, if so, I think she should have stayed home and reached him by telephone."

Whether Stanwyck was sedated or drinking on her visits to the Taylor ranch no one knew for sure. It was a difficult and sad time for her—the horrible end of the life of the man she had loved for thirty-three years.

Taylor was in and out of the hospital nine times during his illness, but on Thursday, June 5, he said his last few words privately to Ronald Reagan: "I only have one request right now. Tell Ursula, be happy."

On Saturday, June 7, 1969, newsmen reported that Robert Taylor was fighting for his life. The following morning Ursula and Art stood over him. The nurse who said she prayed she would not be on duty when Bob died was so upset she was unable to take his blood pressure. Art had to take over, but it really didn't matter.

Robert Taylor closed his eyes.

The next day, June 8, part of Barbara Stanwyck died, too. Was it possible that she had outlived this beautiful man—the young "Mr. Artique" she was so happy to find out was Mr. R. T., her blind date for the evening? The innocent kid from Nebraska who called her every day from England with proposals of marriage and hanging up in a huff only to call back again.

There were so few like Taylor left. Clark Gable, Gary Cooper, Dick Powell, Humphrey Bogart, Tyrone Power, Errol Flynn, Alan Ladd—all untimely deaths.

At first Barbara was sure she would not attend Bob's funeral. She could not bear it. Ursula offered her the courtesy of sitting with the family in the private vestible hidden from the other mourners, but Barbara made it known she would not attend. On Monday she felt the same way, but on Tuesday she changed her mind. Taylor had discussed death with her during their marriage and said, "Don't wear black to my funeral."

Barbara knew she had to attend the memorial service for the man she would love for the rest of her life; she would wear a light-colored dress to honor his deepest feelings about his own death.

But her thoughts drifted back to why she should not go. The funerals of Hollywood celebrities always drew a crowd of fans or curious people, making a circus of a sol-

emn occasion. Perhaps by her very presence there would
be more than the usual disturbance. But she was informed
that Ursula wanted a very private service at Forest Lawn
Cemetery in Glendale. It would be impossible to get
through the main gate without authorization. Relieved
there would be no crowds, Barbara decided to say her
own final farewell to Bob.

Stanwyck, the professional and dedicated actress who
was always early on the set was pathetically late arriving
at the chapel. The mourners were all seated. Ronald Reagan was ready to give the eulogy. The organist was playing the last song. Then she appeared at the back of the
chapel, two men holding her up by each arm.

The bright-yellow dress in itself was startling, but
more shocking was the realization that it was Barbara
Stanwyck being guided down the aisle to a pew. Purvis
thought she was drunk. Art Reeves, remembering her
visits to the ranch, gave Barbara the benefit of the doubt
and felt she was heavily sedated. Regardless of her condition, there was nothing anyone could do about her pathetic appearance. She sat very still until Reagan broke
down half way through the eulogy. He composed himself
and continued, but Barbara wept uncontrollably.

"Today I am sure there is sorrow among the rugged
men in the Northwest who run the swift water of the
Rogue River and who knew him as one of them," Reagan
said. "There are cowpokes up in the valley of Wyoming
who remember him and mourn—mourn a man who rode
and hunted with them. And millions and millions of people who knew him by way of the silver screen. And they
remember with gratitude that in the darkened theater he
never embarrassed them in front of their children.

"I know that some night on the late late show I'm going
to see Bob resplendent in white tie and tails at Delmon-
icos, and I'm sure I'll smile—smile at Robert Spangler
Arlington Brugh Taylor, because I'll remember how a

fellow named Bob really preferred blue jeans and boots. And I'll see him squinting through the smoke of a barbecue as I have seen him a hundred times."

Reagan turned to Ursula, Tessa, and Terry in the hidden vestibule and continued, "In a little while the hurt will be gone. Time will do that for you. Then you will find you can bring out your memories. You can look at them—take comfort from their warmth. As the years go by, you will be very proud. Not so much of the things that we have talked about here—you are going to be proud of the simple things. Things not so stylish in certain circles today, but that just makes them a little more rare and of greater value. Simple things like honor and honesty, responsibility to those he worked for and who worked for him, standing up for what he believed and, yes, even a simple old-fashioned love for his country, and above all, an inner humility."

Barbara tried hard to restrain herself but she could do nothing to dam her overflowing sobs and tears. Yes, she was very conspicuous.

The concern of everyone mourning Taylor's death went beyond the loss of a friend. Only two weeks ago Ursula's son by a former marriage was found dead from an overdose of drugs. She fainted when she discovered his body on her way to see Bob at the hospital. The strain on Ursula was too much, but through the misery and shock her mind was on Bob because she knew that if she were not with him at the end, she wouldn't forgive herself. Yet she had to bury her son.

Taylor was told of Michael's death, and he insisted on coming home one last time after the boy's funeral. Somehow Ursula and Art managed to sneak him out of Saint John's Hospital to the ranch without reporters finding out.

After Michael's death, Bob gave up his own fight; he realized that Ursula would be relieved of an overwhelming burden. Michael was never mentally stable, and whatever life he had was wasted. Taylor rarely allowed him in his home and, when he did, his hippie friends were not admitted.

Ursula had done all she could and Bob knew that, but he worried. Now there was no need to be concerned. Taylor wanted, above all, for his wife to be happy. Referring to Michael, Art Reeves said, "You can't straighten out a crooked tree."

On Thursday, June 5, Taylor returned to the hospital. After Ursula went to Terry's grade school graduation, she rushed back to her husband's bedside. Friends did all they could to help during this trying time. But it was Ursula, the wife and mother, who had to carry the burden by herself and she carried it well.

Now, in the little chapel, they felt she deserved reverence and peace at last. Barbara Stanwyck, unfortunately, was a disturbance, but everyone else remained quiet for Ursula's sake. Purvis, grief-stricken and close to tears himself, was livid. "Why?" he asked repeatedly. "Why did she have to disrupt things?"

Purvis had only met Barbara once or twice and admittedly did not know much about her. He could only judge by what he saw that day in the chapel. Several of Bob's close friends told Purvis Barbara knew what she was doing by portraying the "other widow" and proving to the world for the last time that there will be no other man in her life.

When the brief service was over, she stood up in a faint and had to be helped out of the church, but then managed to walk to her car alone.

It was Ursula who invited Barbara to Ursulor Rancho for "a drink on Bob" with the others—a Hollywood tradition often described as a "dignified wake." It is a time to remember the good times and, for those who had never met in the past or might never see each other again, to share fond memories of the departed friend they knew in common.

While the others mingled, Barbara sat quietly respond-
ing to a few acquaintances. Then she was gone. Purvis
said, "We all gave a sigh of relief until someone saw Barbara taking a stroll with Ursula round and round the circular driveway." Barbara was doing all the talking. Ursula
nodded and listened. The others peeked out from behind
curtains to make sure Ursula was all right. Finally Barbara's car disappeared down the dusty driveway to Mandeville Canyon Road.

Reeves felt Bob would not have appreciated Barbara's
coming to the funeral or to his home. But Ursula, the op-
timist and the forgiver, had extended her hand to the first
Mrs. Robert Taylor.

"But a year later," Reeves explained, "Ursula came
running across the front lawn screaming, 'Damn! Damn!
Damn!' I never heard her swear. Seems she just found out
from her business manager that Barbara had been billing
Taylor for alimony until the day he died. Doctors and
hospital bills had eaten up every cent of cash Taylor had.
It just never occurred to him that Barbara would not make
an exception during the nine months he was so ill. Ursula
finally found out about Barbara the hard way what Bob
had tried to tell her all along.

"When she came screaming to the barn and hysterically
tried to tell me, Ursula became very sick," Reeves said.
"She threw up and broke out in hives. Bob's psychologist
came right over and calmed her by explaining Barbara's
actions—her way of possessing him to the very end. It
wasn't the money, but it might have been the principle.
Ursula, of course, felt used because she had tried to in-
clude Barbara and make her feel wanted.

"Word spread around Hollywood like a prairie fire. It
had been a well-guarded secret that Bob was paying alimony to Barbara. It was a double impact when everyone
found out the poor guy was paying up—until his last
breath."

*   *   *

Stanwyck was a favorite in the fan magazines after Taylor's death. The story of her earlier marriage to Pretty Boy Taylor was exciting reading for the younger crowd. One movie magazine, however, went all out with an article about Barbara's building a shrine to Bob in her home. The magazine offered a lurid picture: that after the funeral she put on the nightgown she wore on her honeymoon with Taylor; that she hung pictures of him throughout the house and ran his movies over and over and over; that faithfully she wore only the jewelry he had given her. This last statement is true, and it's a fact that she still cherishes their wedding pictures. But for the rest?

Friends said the article was terribly exaggerated, but she does cling to keepsakes. And she mourned Taylor's death as if she were the widow, just as she had mourned their divorce. Barbara has repeatedly refused to discuss him and swore that she would never write her memoirs because she would have to relive too many painful and unhappy experiences. Writers and reporters have approached her, but the answers were always the same: "It was so long ago," or "I couldn't bear it."

Dion Fay talked to the press when Taylor died and said, "He was a nice guy. I always referred to him as Gentleman Bob because that described him best."

Whenever Dion came up in the news, reporters naturally approached Barbara. She avoided the subject, usually remaining silent, but in one interview said that some kids are born with bad blood just like horses. When a parent has done everything possible, the only solution is to "save yourself."

In 1970 Stanwyck starred in ABC's Movie of the Week *The House That Wouldn't Die* with Richard Egan. She was splendid as the woman living in a haunted house, and at the age of sixty-three Barbara was on the set earlier than anyone else and still insisted on doing her own stunts. Her stand-in said, "Miss Stanwyck was one star who requested a stand-in and stunt girl because it provided us with work. Simple as that. Show business is tough enough without making it tougher. Most stars use stand-ins or stunt people for long shots or when the photographer is lighting the set. Miss Stanwyck did not enjoy sitting still. She was one of the few actresses who stood on her feet while the lighting director was setting up. This is a very tiring and boring procedure, but Miss Stanwyck was a perfectionist."

Aaron Spelling, the producer of *The House That Wouldn't Die,* asked Barbara to work for him again in *A Taste of Evil,* another ABC Movie of the Week in 1971. With Barbara Parkins and Roddy McDowall, Stanwyck portrays Parkins's mother, who tries to have her daughter committed to an institution so that she can collect an inheritance she feels is rightfully hers.

A Taste of Evil was a genuine Stanwyck movie, her tough-woman role typical of those that had made her popular in the forties.

In November 1971 Barbara began "Fitzgerald and Pride," the pilot for a potential television series about a woman lawyer and her young partner, played by James Stacy. On the second day of shooting Barbara wasn't feeling well, but got through the day. When she arrived home, the pains in her left side were so severe she asked Nancy Sinatra to drive her to Saint John's Hospital. Tests showed a ruptured kidney wall and within hours Barbara underwent emergency surgery for the removal of one kidney. The next day doctors said that although the operation was a success, she would have to remain in the hospital for two weeks. "For two days I was on the other side," Barbara told her friends. "It's very cold there and it's very dark. Thank God, I came back."

Barbara had to back out of "Fitzgerald and Pride."

Susan Hayward replaced her, a difficult task for anyone. "No actress likes to get a great part this way," Hayward said. "I've never met Barbara Stanwyck, but it's a hell of a job trying to fit into her shoes!" Then she sent twelve dozen roses to the hospital.

Ironically Hayward soon discovered she had cancerous brain tumors and did not have long to live. Barbara recovered. Susan did not. After their warm meeting in 1974, Susan took a turn for the worse and died the following year in March.

Stanwyck said, "I am very fortunate under the circumstances. Plenty of people survive with one kidney. I'll be fine."

Aaron Spelling wanted Barbara for *The Letters*, another ABC Movie of the Week, and she felt well enough to begin filming in January 1973. The story dealt with letters lost in a plane crash and delivered a year later. The movie consisted of three mini-stories: John Forsythe starred in the first, Barbara in the second, and Ida Lupino in the third.

The Letters did not receive good reviews, but Stanwyck and Lupino were praised by the critics. If Barbara's fans expected to see an elderly sickly star still recuperating from a serious operation, they were delightfully surprised. She never looked better. And there was a different air about her. Facing death and adjusting to a slower pace, Stanwyck had reached new depths in her acting. She had had a soul-searching experience that brought her closer to God. For once in her life she had to give in to the expertise and perfection of others: her doctors and nurses. This time Stanwyck could not stand-in for them.

On April 28, 1973, a radiant and proud Barbara Stanwyck was inducted into the Hall of Fame of Great Western Performers in the Museum of the National Cowboy Hall of Fame. The candlelit black tie ceremony was held in Oklahoma City, and it was old costar Joel McCrea who gave her the Wrangler Award. Memories were all around her that night. Robert Taylor had been given the same award posthumously—the only nonliving trustee of the museum.

"Always close to Taylor," a friend remarked about her. "He did a Western series on TV. She did, too. She only liked race horses before she met him and couldn't ride worth a damn. When he made Western movies, so did she. Bob said if he had a choice to live another life, it would be in the Old West. So did she. He made the Cowboy Hall of Fame. So did she. He loved guns and she couldn't bear to have them in their house. Then she learned to use them like a professional. I don't think it had anything to do with competition. Not at all. It was closeness—the feeling of sharing or being in the same place, for the same purpose. A bond."

Barbara said the night she received the Wrangler Award in Oklahoma City was one of the most rewarding in her whole career. She described the film clips shown later in the evening. "It started out in the forties when I was young and it went bang, bang, bang—very fast with still photos and a man narrating. Then it moved into the actual film clips. Whoever edited this did a sensational job because when they started shooting the stunts, it looked as if I was breaking my ass and my neck. The people oohed and aahed. It was quite stirring!"

Barbara was finally receiving the awards and honors long overdue, but the grueling fourteen-hour days were over. She moved into a smaller house in the Trousdale Estates area of Beverly Hills and spent her days decorating, watching television, and keeping busy with household chores for a change. It was impossible for her to do nothing, and if a waxed floor was her accomplishment for the day, she accepted it as such.

Stanwyck said her greatest mistake in life was not returning to the Broadway stage when she was still married to Frank Fay. She put the blame partially on trying to hold her marriage together, but if she had to do it all over again, Barbara would have found a way to continue her career in the legitimate theater. "I wouldn't lie about the offers I've had," she said regrettably. "It's so sad because I'd do it if I only had the courage. The fear of facing a live audience in a play is so overwhelming that it seems almost impossible that I was once so unafraid."

Was her marriage the only reason she did not return to the stage?

"No," she sighed. "I fell in love with films. That's a pretty strong reason, isn't it?"

Stanwyck had not been seen on television in four years (except in movie reruns and the syndicated "The Big Valley"), but the seventy-one-year-old actress looked at least a decade younger when she attended the Academy Awards on April 3, 1978. Wearing a rhinestone-studded black gown and looking slimmer than most of the younger actresses, Stanwyck was asked to present one of the awards.

Master of Ceremonies Bob Hope said, "There's a lot of gold being given out tonight, but Hollywood will never run out of it as long as we have treasures like the next two stars. He made his sensational screen debut in *Golden Boy,* and we'll never forget his leading lady whose performances are never less than twenty-four karat. The Golden Boy and his Golden Girl are together again tonight. William Holden and Barbara Stanwyck."

Holden, who was fighting a losing battle with alcohol, would be dead in three years. As he stood next to Barbara, who was eleven years older, Holden looked haggard and worn out. She outshined him without even trying. They adored each other—one reason he decided not to follow the script that night. "Before Barbara and I present the next award, I'd like to say something. Thirty-nine years ago this month, we were working in a film together called *Golden Boy.* It wasn't going well because I was going to be replaced. But due to this lovely human being and her interest and understanding and her professional integrity and her encouragement and, above all, her generosity, I'm here tonight."

Barbara was overwhelmed by the applause. Tears filling her eyes, she tried to talk, but all that came out was: "Oh, Bill!" Then they embraced and she cried for a moment before taking a deep breath and reading the nominations. There was a slight hesitation before she handed him the envelope and said, "And here, Golden Boy, you read it."

In 1981 the Film Society of Lincoln Center wanted to pay tribute to Barbara Stanwyck and her movies. She thought the idea was nice, but her reply was: "We'll see." Obviously she was stalling. Friends hounded her until she finally gave in.

"I could understand if they picked Katharine Hepburn," she told Rex Reed, "but of course she wouldn't do it. But when they asked me, I thought at first it was a mistake. I thought they got me mixed up with Bette Davis. Attention embarrasses me. I do not like to be on display. I was always an extrovert in my work, but when it comes time to be myself, I'll take a powder every time. The woman who came to the airport to meet me couldn't find me because I was hiding behind a post. I never got an Oscar. I never had an acting lesson. Life was my only training. Eighty-five movies, yes. But that wasn't eighty-five great movies, honey. There was some real clinkers in there. Oh, Lord, yes."

On April 13, 1981, Barbara Stanwyck arrived at Avery Fisher Hall with her Golden Boy, William Holden. Looking every bit the great actress and star, she wore a silver sequin gown and white mink stole, brilliant complements to her beautiful white hair.

Henry Fonda was too ill to be there, but he sent a telegram: "Dear Barbara: Can't be at your marvelous evening because I'm having hospital tests. I'm feeling fine but my only sadness is not being able to be with you at the Film Society of Lincoln Center tribute. Shirley approves of my forty-year love for you, Barbara, and she and I will be honoring you in California. We send our very special love."

President Ronald Reagan sent a telegram, too, ending with, "Long before it was fashionable, you were a paradigm of independence and self-direction for women all over the world."

After a standing ovation, Barbara gave a brief speech: "When the Film Society first notified me about this stunt, I thought they made a mistake. I thought they meant Barbra Streisand. Well, we got that straightened out. And then I thought that I had to tell them that I had never won an Academy Award. So we got that straightened out, too. They said that didn't make any difference to them." Wanting the crowd who had gathered in her honor to know she hadn't gotten there alone, she thanked everyone who had helped and guided her throughout the years. She was especially appreciative of being chosen for the tribute, which she described as "a beautiful memory."

Being seen around Hollywood and New York with her Golden Boy William Holden was a rebirth for Barbara. He had been in the public eye while romancing Stephanie Powers, who, as star of the popular television series "Hart to Hart," was far more interesting news than Barbara Stanwyck. His fans had no idea how serious his drinking problem was, and that this affliction was the reason Powers had postponed their wedding many times. But the public was cheering for Holden to win this beautiful new star. Barbara, indirectly, shared in the limelight, praying and cheering the loudest for Holden.

Stanwyck and Holden attended a small dinner party in the fall of 1981. The other guests said Barbara was listening to Bill's complaint about the lack of good scripts in

Hollywood. He thought at last he had found one, *That Championship Season;* he was eager to get started, but after many delays the outlook seemed dim. "Of course, he always talked about Africa," one dinner guest said, "and told us he would retire there. But Bill didn't look happy. Stephanie had put their affair on hold until he stopped drinking. She kept in touch, but they weren't together."

Less than a month following that intimate dinner party Barbara was viciously awakened one night by a masked burglar. "He was wearing a ski mask," she said, "and he had a gun. He wanted to know where I hid my money and jewelry. I was terrified and in shock, so I told him. I tried to turn on the bedside lamp and he shouted, 'I told you not to look or I'll kill you!' and he hit me over the head with the gun before he pushed me into a closet. The blood was running down my face, but somehow I managed to put my hand against the sliding door so it wasn't shut tight. He told me if I tried to get out he'd kill me."

The thief was over six feet tall and weighed about two hundred pounds. She said, "I was dizzy and on the verge of passing out, but I was determined not to bleed to death in the closet. Thank God, I was able to think straight and put my thumb in the door. I waited and waited. My blood was staining the carpet in the closet and I was losing consciousness, but I had to hang on."

When all was silent, she stumbled from the closet and called the police. The loss of jewelry and money was estimated at only $5,000, but the jewelry was worth a fortune in memories, which no amount of money could replace. Aside from diamond earrings and a necklace, the greatest loss was a cigarette box and pieces of jewelry that Taylor had given her.

A neighbor said, "We were all very surprised that a robbery with such violence should occur in this quiet area. We've never been bothered before. Police said it was

unusual. The thief broke a window to get into Miss Stanwyck's house. It was a horrible experience for her, being
roughed up and having a flashlight in her eyes. He didn't
have to pistol-whip such a small and frail woman. Even
though her head required only a few stitches, she said she
could never be the same again. Then she told me how destroyed she was over losing the jewelry and a gold and
platinum cigarette box that Robert had given her. She
never stopped loving him. Her bruises and cuts will heal,
but she can never replace those gifts that she treasured
above everything else."

Before Barbara was beaten and robbed, she was beginning a new social life and loving it. She told her neighbor,
"I never had time to relax. My whole life was my career.
Then I got sick and almost died. After that things
changed." Stanwyck went on to say how wonderful it was
shopping for gowns and shoes and getting her luxurious
furs out of storage. She began participating in Hollywood
benefits and award banquets. Old friends asked her out
for dinner. Critics raved about her figure and her wardrobe. Most astounding was how young she looked. No
one believed she could possibly be seventy-four years old.

Young starlets were amazed and more than a little envi-
ous. "There are hundreds of diet and exercise fads in Hollywood," one ingenue moaned, "and I've tried them all,
but I doubt I'll ever look as good as Barbara Stanwyck!"

The Queen sat on her throne alone. There were few
movie legends left and those who were alive preferred to
stay out of the Hollywood glare. Barbara had reversed the
star system by basking in the social spotlight after proving
her greatness as an actress; that is, until she was beaten
and robbed.

Terrified of leaving her house, but just as afraid of
locking herself in, Barbara paid over $10,000 to have an
electronic security system installed. Every noise frightened her. When she found out that the thief had had an

accomplice that night, she became even more concerned and worried. She feared one or both would come back.

Ten years earlier she had been harassed by an "admirer" who lurked in the bushes near her front door and jumped out to greet her at all hours. But after weeks of this annoyance Barbara had the man arrested. She appeared at the hearing, but since he had not technically committed a crime, he was set free—only to return to her house. She found him asleep in her garden and sent him away. "He told me he would return," she said, "and he did, but this time he was trying to cut through my screen door. The police took him away again, but I was forced to move."

After that episode, Barbara thought the Trousdale Estates would afford her privacy and safety. But could she forget the horrible nightmare of waking up and finding a man standing over her with a gun? And could she forget that ten years ago the police were powerless to help her and couldn't even arrest a lunatic who lingered near her house day and night?

Now she was terrified to leave home. Rarely did she go out for dinner unless her escort met her at the front door, looked after her—almost guarded her—all evening, and then returned her home safely behind the bolted door before he left.

Already nervous and distraught, Barbara nearly collapsed when she received a telephone call on November 16: William Holden had been found dead in his Shoreham Towers apartment. Obviously drunk, he had fallen and hit his head on the end of a table. Golden Boy had bled to death alone at the age of sixty-three.

William Holden's tragic death was a shock, and the nagging questions everyone asked: "How could a famous star bleed to death all alone? He had so many friends. And why was he drinking so heavily all alone?"

It was a stark realization that living alone can be dangerous, regardless of how famous or rich you are. Stanwyck and Holden had suffered from the same heartaches. Neither could have the one they loved. Neither could bring back the great films of the Golden Era. Neither wanted to live alone. Drink alone. Think alone.

Two weeks later Natalie Wood drowned off the shores of Catalina. Again Stanwyck was deeply affected. She had encouraged and helped Natalie's husband, Robert Wagner, thirty years ago, and he went on to become a famous and successful actor. Ironically, Wagner costarred with Holden's love, Stephanie Powers, in "Hart to Hart." Wagner was aboard the yacht when Natalie screamed for help only a few feet from the anchor. Stephanie had left Holden. Both stars felt tremendous guilt that they had lost their chances to save the ones they loved most.

The two young men Barbara had chosen to help and who had, in turn, fallen in love with her had gone through much grieving and pain as a result of fame and money. She wondered if it was all worth it.

Several weeks later she was rushed to the hospital with pneumonia; she was also suffering from an enlarged liver. On February 2, 1982, doctors said it was touch and go. For three days she was in serious condition in the intensive care unit at Saint John's Hospital, but on February 5, much improved, she was moved to a private room.

She told reporters on the telephone, "They treated me with antibiotics. I've made the turnaround in my recovery. Now I want to work again."

David Wolper, one of the producers of *The Thorn Birds*, wanted to know if Barbara was serious.

"The role of Mary Carson in *The Thorn Birds* was the best I have read in two years," Stanwyck said, and she agreed to do the miniseries for television.

Unfortunately the script was not as good as Colleen McCullough's best-selling novel. According to McCullough, producers Wolper and Stan Margulies had taken the bitch out of Mary Carson—and was Stanwyck furious! She made a phone call to the producers, warning them she was angry as hell. The part of the rich bitch who is obsessed with a young priest and tries to destroy him when he does not respond to her is a touchy one, Barbara admitted to them, but she had accepted the role based on the character in the book—not some wishy-washy dame who gives up without a fight. Although she should not have accepted the role without a finished script, she would honor her contract, but with great disappointment. She slammed down the phone in a huff.

This conversation has never been totally revealed. Producers Wolper and Margulies were in shock; Stanwyck's vocabulary made their hair stand up straight and "hair grow where there wasn't any!" They did, however, review the script and decided Barbara was right. Mary Carson reverted to the bitch, and Barbara Stanwyck reverted to the lamb.

Despite her second close brush with death in February, Barbara had every reason to get well quickly because the Academy of Motion Picture Arts and Sciences announced it would present a special Oscar for her long and distinguished acting career. The young actor John Travolta, who resembled the youthful Robert Taylor, was proud to introduce her at the ceremonies:

> Four years ago William Holden and Barbara Stanwyck came up on this stage to present an award. When they did, Mr. Holden departed from the script to speak from his heart. He said that his career derived from the lady standing next to him. All he was came from her generosity, her support, and her abiding belief in him. Barbara was completely surprised by this. She listened, her public face letting her private face show, but just for an instant. The actress in control, and that's the very essence of Barbara Stanwyck's eminence and that hold she has on the audience. She's reality. She's professional and, when she walks across the screen, it's beauty and confidence. She's always the woman she plays and yet always herself.

The theater lights were turned down as film clips from some of Stanwyck's most notable films were shown: *The Lady Eve, Annie Oakley, Double Indemnity, Sorry, Wrong Number, Golden Boy,* and *Stella Dallas.* The audience was in tears as they watched poor Stella, dressed in rags, peering through a window from the street to catch a last glimpse of her daughter being married in a society wedding—and then a policeman telling Stella to move along.

"Ladies and gentlemen, Miss Barbara Stanwyck!"

Wearing a clinging sequined fire-engine-red gown, she walked onstage to a standing ovation, which lasted over a minute. A calm expression on her face, Stanwyck strode in with the gallant walk of a panther and accepted the applause that was so long overdue. There was humbleness and gratitude and patience in her eyes, but there was also satisfaction, mixed with the disappointment that over the past forty years she had never been given the Academy Award when she had rightly deserved it—especially those times sitting in the audience with Robert Taylor and yearning to run up to the stage breathlessly for her acceptance speech. But her time had finally come.

> Thank you. Thank you very much. I'd like to thank the Board of Governors of the Academy for giving me this special award. I . . . I tried many times to get it, but I didn't make it. So this is indeed very special to me. You don't get them alone. There were writers, directors, producers—all their kindnesses to me through the many years. And the people backstage. The remarkable crews that we have the privilege of working with. The electricians, the property men, the stagehands . . . oh . . . camera . . . they're just marvelous. And *my* wonderful group, the stunt men and the women who taught me so well. I'm grateful to them and I thank them very much.
>
> A few years ago I stood on this stage with William Holden, as a presenter. I loved him very much, and I miss him.

He always wished that I would get an Oscar, and so tonight, my Golden Boy, you got your wish.

It was quite apparent that she was weeping during
those last few words—not for the Oscar, which she had
finally won, but for Bill Holden.

Another emotional moment for Barbara that night was
the announcement that her dear friend Henry Fonda had
won the award for best actor in *On Golden Pond*. He was
too ill to attend the ceremonies, so his daughter, Jane, accepted the Oscar for him. It was just a matter of months
for Fonda.

The year 1982 would be contradictory one of illness,
hard work, and further recognition for Barbara Stanwyck.
In June she began filming *The Thorn Birds* with Richard
Chamberlain, Jean Simmons, Richard Kiley, Christopher
Plummer, and Rachel Ward.

Her stand-in reported a familiar story: "Miss Stanwyck
could still ride a horse. As a matter of fact, she kept up
with the rest of us. Everyone would have understood if
she had gotten tired because she was seventy-five. She
was remarkable not only because she surpassed herself
this time, as Mary Carson, but because the makeup people
had to put special plastic on her face to make her look
older! We all wanted to know her beauty secrets. She said
she ate the right foods and got plenty of rest. Someone
said she had a treadmill in her bedroom and she walked a
mile uphill everyday."

Although Barbara did not take the chances she usually
did, in the house-burning scene the smoke was thicker
than expected and she inhaled too much smoke. Typically
she remained until the end of the day before going to
Santa Monica Hospital, where the doctors discovered she
was in serious, although not critical, condition. Doctors
insisted she remain for three weeks to take breathing ex-
ercises with a deep-breath inhalator. She was then put on

medication and released. She told reporters, "It was nothing, really, but the smoke aggravated a respiratory problem I've had for a while."

Although Barbara was in and out of the hospital four times while working on *The Thorn Birds*, she completed her role of Mary Carson brilliantly opposite Richard Chamberlain. Her final words in the miniseries were like a summation of all that made Barbara Stanwyck the great actress—and woman—she was: "Let me tell you something, Cardinal de Bricassart, about old age and about that God of yours. That vengeful God who ruins our bodies and leaves us with only enough wit for regret. Inside this stupid body I am still young. I still feel. I still want. I still dream and I still love you. Oh, God, how much!"

She closes the door in his face and commits suicide.

Stanwyck was nominated for an Emmy in 1983.

Ten

"Happiness is within yourself," she once told Rex Reed. "Get ready for the dream to fade. So I'm no longer in demand, but so what? I see no reason to go into decline or hit the bottle or sink into a melancholy depression. I've had my time and it was lovely. I'm grateful for it. Now I have to move aside and make room for somebody else. I'm not jealous of anybody. Well, I take it back. Maybe Miss Hepburn because she won three Academy Awards. But sing no sad songs for Barbara Stanwyck. What the hell! Whatever I had, it worked, didn't it?"

As for her personal life, she was resigned to that, too. It was hard getting used to living alone for the first two years, she admitted. Now she could not imagine living with anyone because she had her own routine. She couldn't imagine why reporters would want to talk to her anymore. She didn't have a regular job or a steady boy-friend. "Who the hell cares?" she sighed.

Obviously Dion Fay did.

In 1984 he granted an interview and spoke very freely about his adopted mother, begging her to see him. "She hasn't been well," he said, "and I think it's time, after thirty-one years, to make peace."

Dion claimed he never got the love, respect, and support he needed as a child, and later, when he grew up, hadn't seen his mother as often as he wanted to. He was now fifty-one and he pleaded for a chance to get together with his mother and make things better.

Dion also had memories of his father, Frank Fay. "He was a heavy drinker," Dion said, "and he used to beat my mother. They had brutal arguments."

Dion felt Barbara was disappointed because he had not turned out to be special. "I was fat, had freckles all over my face and wore glasses. I was awkward, too," he said in the interview.

Dion said that, when he was fifteen, Barbara demanded he attend a military school fifteen hundred miles away. That was the beginning of the end, he said. For the previous ten years he had been only six miles away from his mother and never saw her, so how often would he see her if they were fifteen hundred miles away?

In this 1984 interview Dion Fay admitted he had gotten into trouble, but he blamed it on lack of love and attention, a way of fighting back. But for the past twenty years he feels he has been a model citizen and asks forgiveness.

But true to form, Barbara Stanwyck had no comment.

She had turned back only once—to Robert Taylor after his widely publicized affair in Rome. She had forgiven him and was willing to try again. She never complained that she was wrong. She was open about her feelings for Bob, regardless of what he had said or done.

As for Dion Fay, it seems unlikely this reunion will take place.

For those who still view Barbara Stanwyck's movies at film festivals and on television and for those who remember paying to see her on the first-run movie screen, she remains one of Hollywood's true legends. One of the greatest. She gave everything—love, guts, talent, time, devotion and even her health—in order to become one of the best actresses in Hollywood. Yet she never won an Oscar when she deserved it. If she paid the price, she has no regrets. It was her choice, after all.

She was an orphan, a hoofer, Broadway's pride. She was often shunned by Hollywood, despite three nominations for the Oscar and two Emmys. But there was always applause from her coworkers. Regardless of her rigorous professional standards, she was able to enforce them without making too many enemies. Off the set, however, is another story that will go, for the most part, untold.

She is not one to regret much or dwell upon how she might do it over—only maybe a few scripts that turned out poorly.

She never lost her Brooklyn accent or the sharp tongue that had to fight the other kids on the dirty streets because she was an orphan. With all of her grace and sophistication, she's the first one to remind you where she came from. And she learned the hard way that Hollywood was the toughest town of them all.

"Veni! Vide! Vici!"

Postscript

*T*he year 1985 brought both joy and tragedy to Barbara Stanwyck.

On June 21, she watched in stunned silence while seven fire engines arrived to control an attic fire that gutted her $3 million home. Firemen held her back as she rushed for the front door, pleading with them to let her save irreplaceable mementos—love letters written to her by Robert Taylor and personal photos of their life together. Friends said these faded treasures were more precious to her than her valuable art collection. The firemen remarked, "Miss Stanwyck was a brave lady through it all—especially her attempts to risk her life for a few love letters and pictures."

At the time she was negotiating with ABC and the producers of "Dynasty" to play Charlton Heston's sister Constance Colby Patterson in "Dynasty II: The Colbys," a weekly TV series to make its debut in November 1985. But, the producers wondered, was the seventy-eight-year-old Barbara Stanwyck up to this after being in ill health and suffering through the fire?

Absolutely! She will be reunited with her "Big Valley" TV daughter, Linda Evans, and will be viewed by still another generation who will be moved by her presence on the screen, but not in western garb this time. Barbara Stanwyck will face the camera wearing jewel-studded gowns and diamonds, thus continuing her life and career with yet another acting assignment, yet another triumph for this great, proud actress.

BROADWAY NIGHTS   (First National, 1927)
PRODUCER: Robert Kane
DIRECTOR: Joseph C. Boyle
SCREENPLAY: Forrest Halsey
CAST: Sam Hardy, Lois Wilson, Louis John Bar-
tels, Philip Strange, Barbara Stanwyck

THE LOCKED DOOR   (United Artists, 1930)
PRODUCER: George Fitzmaurice
DIRECTOR: George Fitzmaurice
SCREENPLAY: C. Gardner Sullivan
CAST: William Boyd, Barbara Stanwyck, Rod La
Rocque, Betty Bronson, ZaSu Pitts, Harry
Stubbs

MEXICALI ROSE   (Columbia, 1930)
PRODUCER: Harry Cohn
DIRECTOR: Erle C. Kenton
SCREENPLAY: Gladys Lehman
CAST: Sam Hardy, Barbara Stanwyck, William
Janney, Arthur Rankin, Louis King

LADIES OF LEISURE　(Columbia, 1930)
PRODUCER: Harry Cohn
DIRECTOR: Frank Capra
SCREENPLAY: Jo Swerling
CAST: Barbara Stanwyck, Lowell Sherman, Ralph Graves, Marie Provost, Nance O'Neil, George Fawcett

ILLICIT　(Warner Brothers, 1931)
PRODUCER: Warner Brothers
DIRECTOR: Archie Mayo
SCREENPLAY: Harvey Thew
CAST: Barbara Stanwyck, Ricardo Cortez, Charles Butterworth, James Rennie, Joan Blondell

TEN CENTS A DANCE　(Columbia, 1931)
PRODUCER: Harry Cohn
DIRECTOR: Lionel Barrymore
SCREENPLAY: Jo Swerling
CAST: Barbara Stanwyck, Ricardo Cortez, Sally Blane, Monroe Owsley, Blanche Friderici, David Newell

NIGHT NURSE　(Warner Brothers, 1931)
DIRECTOR: Willam A. Wellman
SCREENPLAY: Oliver H. P. Garrett
CAST: Barbara Stanwyck, Joan Blondell, Clark Gable, Charles Winninger, Ben Lyon, Blanche Friderici, Edward Nugent

THE MIRACLE WOMAN　(Columbia, 1931)
PRODUCER: Harry Cohn
DIRECTOR: Frank Capra
SCREENPLAY: Jo Swerling
CAST: Barbara Stanwyck, Sam Hardy, David Manners, Beryl Mercer, Charles Middleton, Eddie Boland, Russell Hopton

FORBIDDEN (Columbia, 1932)
PRODUCER: Harry Cohn
DIRECTOR: Frank Capra
SCREENPLAY: Frank Capra, Jo Swerling
CAST: Barbara Stanwyck, Adolphe Menjou, Ralph Bellamy, Thomas Jefferson, Dorothy Peterson, Myrna Fresholt

SHOPWORN (Columbia, 1932)
DIRECTOR: Nicholas Grinde
SCREENPLAY: Sarah Y. Mason, Jo Swerling, Robert Riskin
CAST: Barbara Stanwyck, ZaSu Pitts, Regis Toomey, Lucien Littlefield, Robert Alden, Oscar Apfel, Clara Blandick

SO BIG (Warner Brothers, 1932)
DIRECTOR: William A. Wellman
SCREENPLAY: J. Grubb Alexander, Robert Lord
CAST: Barbara Stanwyck, George Brent, Guy Kibbee, Bette Davis, Dickie Moore, Mae Madison, Alan Hale

THE PURCHASE PRICE (Warner Brothers, 1932)
DIRECTOR: William A. Wellman
SCREENPLAY: Robert Lord
CAST: Barbara Stanwyck, George Brent, Lyle Talbot, Hardie Albright, David Landau, Leila Bennett, Matt McHugh

THE BITTER TEA OF GENERAL YEN
(Columbia, 1933)
PRODUCER: Walter Wanger
DIRECTOR: Frank Capra

SCREENPLAY: Edward Paramore
CAST: Barbara Stanwyck, Nils Asther, Toshia Mori, Richard Loo, Walter Connolly, Gavin Gordon

LADIES THEY TALK ABOUT   (Warner Brothers, 1933)

DIRECTORS: William Keighley, Howard Bretherton
SCREENPLAY: Sidney Sutherland, Brown Holmes
CAST: Barbara Stanwyck, Preston Foster, Lyle Talbot, Lillian Roth, Dorothy Burgess, Ruth Donnelly

BABY FACE   (Warner Brothers, 1933)

DIRECTOR: Alfred E. Green
SCREENPLAY: Gene Markey, Kathryn Scola
CAST: Barbara Stanwyck, George Brent, Donald Cook, Margaret Lindsay, John Wayne, Arthur Hohl

EVER IN MY HEART   (Warner Brothers, 1933)

DIRECTOR: Archie Mayo
SCREENPLAY: Bertram Milhauser
CAST: Barbara Stanwyck, Ralph Bellamy, Otto Kruger, Ruth Donnelly, Frank Albertson, George Cooper, Wallis Clark

GAMBLING LADY   (Warner Brothers, 1934)

DIRECTOR: Archie Mayo
SCREENPLAY: Ralph Block, Doris Malloy
CAST: Barbara Stanwyck, Joel McCrea, Pat O'Brien, Claire Dodd, Phillip Reed, C. Aubrey Smith, Robert Barrat, Arthur Vinton

A LOST LADY   (First National, 1934)

DIRECTOR: Alfred E. Green
SCREENPLAY: Gene Markey, Kathryn Scola
CAST: Barbara Stanwyck, Ricardo Cortez, Frank

Morgan, Lyle Talbot, Phillip Reed, Hobart Cavanaugh, Henry Kolker

THE SECRET BRIDE   (Warner Brothers, 1935)
DIRECTOR: William Dieterle
SCREENPLAY: Tom Buckingham, F. Hugh Herbert,
Mary McCall, Jr.
CAST: Barbara Stanwyck, Warren William,
Glenda Farrell, Grant Mitchell, Henry
O'Neill, Arthur Byron, Douglas Dum-
brille

THE WOMAN IN RED   (First National, 1935)
DIRECTOR: Robert Florey
SCREENPLAY: Mary McCall, Jr., Peter Milne
CAST: Barbara Stanwyck, Gene Raymond, John
Eldredge, Phillip Reed, Genevieve Tobin,
Arthur Treacher, Russell Hicks

RED SALUTE   (United Artists, 1935)
PRODUCER: Edward Small
DIRECTOR: Sidney Lanfield
SCREENPLAY: Humphrey Pearson, Manuel Seff
CAST: Barbara Stanwyck, Robert Young, Hardie
Albright, Cliff Edwards, Ruth Donnelly,
Gordon Jones, Paul Stanton

ANNIE OAKLEY   (RKO, 1935)
ASSOCIATE
PRODUCER: Cliff Reid
DIRECTOR: George Stevens
SCREENPLAY: Joel Sayre, John Twist
CAST: Barbara Stanwyck, Preston Foster, Mel-
vyn Douglas, Moroni Olsen, Andy Clyde,
Chief Thunder Bird, Pert Kelton

A MESSAGE TO GARCIA   (Twentieth
Century–Fox, 1936)
PRODUCER: Darryl F. Zanuck

DIRECTOR: George Marshall
SCREENPLAY: W. P. Lipscomb, Gene Fowler
CAST: Wallace Beery, Barbara Stanwyck, John Boles, Alan Hale, Herbert Mundin, Mona Barrie, Enrique Acosta

THE BRIDE WALKS OUT (RKO, 1936)

PRODUCER: Edward Small
DIRECTOR: Leigh Jason
SCREENPLAY: P. J. Wolfson, Philip Epstein
CAST: Barbara Stanwyck, Robert Young, Gene Raymond, Ned Sparks, Helen Broderick, Willie Best, Billy Gilbert, Hattie McDaniel

HIS BROTHER'S WIFE (Metro-Goldwyn-Mayer, 1936)

PRODUCER: Lawrence Weingarten
DIRECTOR: W. S. Van Dyke
SCREENPLAY: Leon Gordon, John Meehan
CAST: Barbara Stanwyck, Robert Taylor, Jean Hersholt, Joseph Calleia, John Eldredge, Samuel S. Hinds

BANJO ON MY KNEE (Twentieth Century–Fox, 1936)

PRODUCER: Darryl F. Zanuck
DIRECTOR: John Cromwell
CAST: Barbara Stanwyck, Joel McCrea, Walter Brennan, Buddy Ebsen, Katherine de Mille, Helen Westley, Walter Catlett

THE PLOUGH AND THE STARS (RKO, 1937)

ASSOCIATE
PRODUCERS: Cliff Reid, Robert Sisk
DIRECTOR: John Ford
SCREENPLAY: Dudley Nichols
CAST: Barbara Stanwyck, Preston Foster, Barry

Fitzgerald, Eileen Crowe, Una O'Connor,
Denis O'Dea, Bonita Granville

INTERNES CAN'T TAKE MONEY   (Paramount,
1937)
PRODUCER: Benjamin Glazer
DIRECTOR: Alfred Santell
SCREENPLAY: Rian James, Theodore Reeves
CAST: Barbara Stanwyck, Joel McCrea, Lloyd
Nolan, Lee Bowman, Barry Macollum,
Irving Bacon, Gaylord Pendleton

THIS IS MY AFFAIR   (Twentieth Century-Fox,
1937)
PRODUCER: Darryl F. Zanuck
DIRECTOR: William A. Seiter
SCREENPLAY: Allen Rivkin, Lamar Trotti
CAST: Robert Taylor, Barbara Stanwyck, Victor
McLaglen, Brian Donlevy, Sidney
Blackmer, John Carradine

STELLA DALLAS   (United Artists, 1937)
PRODUCER: Samuel Goldwyn
DIRECTOR: King Vidor
SCREENPLAY: Sarah Y. Mason, Victor Heerman
CAST: Barbara Stanwyck, John Boles, Anne Shir-
ley, Alan Hale, Barbara O'Neil, Marjorie
Main, George Walcott, Tim Holt

BREAKFAST FOR TWO   (RKO, 1937)
PRODUCER: Edward Kaufman
DIRECTOR: Alfred Santell
SCREENPLAY: Charles Kaufman, Paul Yawitz, Viola
Brothers Shore
CAST: Barbara Stanwyck, Herbert Marshall,
Glenda Farrell, Eric Blore, Donald Meek,
Frank M. Thomas

ALWAYS GOOD-BYE (Twentieth Century–Fox, 1938)

PRODUCER: Darryl F. Zanuck
DIRECTOR: Sidney Lanfield
SCREENPLAY: Kathryn Scola, Edith Skouras
CAST: Barbara Stanwyck, Herbert Marshall, Ian Hunter, Cesar Romero, Lynn Bari, Binnie Barnes, Mary Forbes

THE MAD MISS MANTON (RKO, 1938)

PRODUCER: Pandro S. Berman
DIRECTOR: Leigh Jason
SCREENPLAY: Philip G. Epstein
CAST: Barbara Stanwyck, Henry Fonda, Sam Levene, Frances Mercer, Stanley Ridges, Vicki Lester, Ann Evers

UNION PACIFIC (Paramount, 1939)

PRODUCER: Cecil B. De Mille
DIRECTOR: Cecil B. De Mille
SCREENPLAY: Walter DeLeon, C. Gardner Sullivan, Jesse Lasky, Jr.
CAST: Barbara Stanwyck, Joel McCrea, Akim Tamiroff, Robert Preston, Lynne Overman, Brian Donlevy, Anthony Quinn, Evelyn Keyes

GOLDEN BOY (Columbia, 1939)

PRODUCER: William Perlberg
DIRECTOR: Rouben Mamoulian
SCREENPLAY: Lewis Meltzer, Daniel Taradash, Sarah Y. Mason, Victor Heerman
CAST: Barbara Stanwyck, William Holden, Adolphe Menjou, Lee J. Cobb, Sam Levene, Joseph Calleia

REMEMBER THE NIGHT (Paramount, 1940)

PRODUCER: Mitchell Leisen

DIRECTOR: Mitchell Leisen
SCREENPLAY: Preston Sturges
CAST: Barbara Stanwyck, Fred MacMurray, Beulah Bondi, Elizabeth Patterson, Sterling Holloway, Charles Waldron

THE LADY EVE   (Paramount, 1941)
PRODUCER: Paul Jones
DIRECTOR: Preston Sturges
SCREENPLAY: Preston Sturges
CAST: Barbara Stanwyck, Henry Fonda, Charles Coburn, Eugene Pallette, William Demarest, Eric Blore

MEET JOHN DOE   (Warner Brothers/Frank Capra Productions, 1941)
PRODUCER: Frank Capra
DIRECTOR: Frank Capra
SCREENPLAY: Robert Riskin
CAST: Gary Cooper, Barbara Stanwyck, Edward Arnold, Walter Brennan, Spring Byington, James Gleason, Gene Lockhart

YOU BELONG TO ME   (Columbia, 1941)
PRODUCER: Wesley Ruggles
DIRECTOR: Wesley Ruggles
SCREENPLAY: Claude Binyon
CAST: Barbara Stanwyck, Henry Fonda, Edgar Buchanan, Roger Clark, Ruth Donnelly, Melville Cooper, Ralph Peters

BALL OF FIRE   (RKO, 1942)
PRODUCER: Samuel Goldwyn
DIRECTOR: Howard Hawks
SCREENPLAY: Charles Brackett, Billy Wilder
CAST: Gary Cooper, Barbara Stanwyck, Oscar Homolka, Henry Travers, S. Z. Sakall, Tully Marshall, Dana Andrews, Dan Duryea, Allen Jenkins

THE GREAT MAN'S LADY (Paramount, 1942)
PRODUCER: William A. Wellman
DIRECTOR: William A. Wellman
SCREENPLAY: W. L. River
CAST: Barbara Stanwyck, Joel McCrea, Brian Donlevy, Thurston Hall, Katharine Stevens, Lloyd Corrigan, Etta McDaniel

THE GAY SISTERS (Warner Brothers, 1942)
PRODUCER: Henry Blanke
DIRECTOR: Irving Rapper
SCREENPLAY: Lenore Coffee
CAST: Barbara Stanwyck, George Brent, Geraldine Fitzgerald, Donald Crisp, Gig Young, Nancy Coleman, Gene Lockhart

LADY OF BURLESQUE (United Artists, 1943)
PRODUCER: Hunt Stromberg
DIRECTOR: William A. Wellman
SCREENPLAY: James Gunn
CAST: Barbara Stanwyck, Michael O'Shea, J. Edward Bromberg, Iris Adrian, Gloria Dickson, Victoria Faust, Charles Dingle

FLESH AND FANTASY (Universal, 1943)
PRODUCERS: Charles Boyer, Julien Duvivier
DIRECTOR: Julien Duvivier
SCREENPLAY: Ernest Pascal, Samuel Hoffenstein, Ellis St. Joseph
CAST: Edward G. Robinson, Charles Boyer, Barbara Stanwyck, Betty Field, Robert Cummings, Thomas Mitchell, Charles Winninger, Anna Lee, Dame May Whitty, C. Aubrey Smith, Robert Benchley

DOUBLE INDEMNITY (Paramount, 1944)
PRODUCER: Joseph Sistrom
DIRECTOR: Billy Wilder

SCREENPLAY: Billy Wilder, Raymond Chandler
CAST: Fred MacMurray, Barbara Stanwyck, Edward G. Robinson, Porter Hall, Jean Heather, Tom Powers, Byron Barr

HOLLYWOOD CANTEEN   (Warner Brothers, 1944)
PRODUCER: Alex Gottlieb
DIRECTOR: Delmer Daves
SCREENPLAY: Delmer Daves
CAST: Joan Leslie, Robert Hutton, Dane Clark, Janis Paige; Guest appearances: Barbara Stanwyck and other Warner stars

CHRISTMAS IN CONNECTICUT   (Warner Brothers, 1945)
PRODUCER: William Jacobs
DIRECTOR: Peter Godfrey
SCREENPLAY: Lionel Houser, Adele Commandini
CAST: Barbara Stanwyck, Dennis Morgan, Sydney Greenstreet, Reginald Gardiner, S. Z. Sakall, Una O'Connor

MY REPUTATION   (Warner Brothers, 1946)
PRODUCER: Henry Blanke
DIRECTOR: Curtis Bernhardt
SCREENPLAY: Catherine Turney
CAST: Barbara Stanwyck, George Brent, Warner Anderson, Lucile Watson, Eve Arden, Jerome Cowan, Ann Todd

THE BRIDE WORE BOOTS   (Paramount, 1946)
PRODUCER: Seton I. Miller
DIRECTOR: Irving Pichel
SCREENPLAY: Dwight Mitchell Wiley
CAST: Barbara Stanwyck, Robert Cummings, Diana Lynn, Peggy Wood, Patric Knowles, Robert Benchley, Natalie Wood

THE STRANGE LOVE OF MARTHA IVERS
(Paramount, 1946)
PRODUCER: Hal B. Wallis
DIRECTOR: Lewis Milestone
SCREENPLAY: Robert Rossen
CAST: Barbara Stanwyck, Van Heflin, Lizabeth Scott, Kirk Douglas, Judith Anderson, Roman Bohnen, Darryl Hickman, Janis Wilson

CALIFORNIA   (Paramount, 1947)
PRODUCER: Seton I. Miller
DIRECTOR: John Farrow
SCREENPLAY: Frank Butler, Theodore Strauss
CAST: Ray Milland, Barbara Stanwyck, Barry Fitzgerald, Albert Dekker, Anthony Quinn, George Coulouris, Frank Faylen

THE TWO MRS. CARROLLS   (Warner Brothers, 1947)
PRODUCER: Mark Hellinger
DIRECTOR: Peter Godfrey
SCREENPLAY: Thomas Job
CAST: Humphrey Bogart, Barbara Stanwyck, Alexis Smith, Nigel Bruce, Isobel Elsom, Peter Godfrey

THE OTHER LOVE   (United Artists, 1947)
PRODUCER: David Lewis
DIRECTOR: André de Toth
SCREENPLAY: Harry Brown, Ladislas Fodor
CAST: Barbara Stanwyck, David Niven, Richard Conte, Gilbert Roland, Joan Lorring, Lenore Aubert, Maria Palmer

CRY WOLF   (Warner Brothers, 1947)
PRODUCER: Henry Blanke
DIRECTOR: Peter Godfrey
SCREENPLAY: Catherine Turney

CAST: Errol Flynn, Barbara Stanwyck, Richard Basehart, Geraldine Brooks, Jerome Cowan, John Ridgely

VARIETY GIRL   (Paramount, 1947)
PRODUCER: Daniel Dare
DIRECTOR: George Marshall
SCREENPLAY: Edmund Hartmann, Frank Tashlin, Robert Welch, Monte Brice
CAST: Bing Crosby, Bob Hope, Ray Milland, Gary Cooper, Barbara Stanwyck, Alan Ladd, Paulette Goddard, Dorothy Lamour, and most of the Paramount lot

B.F.'S DAUGHTER   (Metro-Goldwyn-Mayer, 1948)
PRODUCER: Edwin H. Knopf
DIRECTOR: Robert Z. Leonard
SCREENPLAY: Luther Davis
CAST: Barbara Stanwyck, Charles Coburn, Van Heflin, Richard Hart, Keenan Wynn, Margaret Lindsay, Spring Byington

SORRY, WRONG NUMBER   (Paramount, 1948)
PRODUCERS: Hal B. Wallis, Anatole Litvak
DIRECTOR: Anatole Litvak
SCREENPLAY: Lucille Fletcher
CAST: Barbara Stanwyck, Burt Lancaster, Wendell Corey, Ann Richards, Ed Begley, Leif Erickson, William Conrad

THE LADY GAMBLES   (Universal, 1949)
PRODUCER: Michel Kraike
DIRECTOR: Michael Gordon
SCREENPLAY: Roy Huggins
CAST: Barbara Stanwyck, Robert Preston, Stephen McNally, Edith Barrett, Leif Erickson, John Hoyt

EAST SIDE, WEST SIDE   (Metro-Goldwyn-Mayer, 1949)

PRODUCER: Voldemar Vetluguin
DIRECTOR: Mervyn LeRoy
SCREENPLAY: Isobel Lennart
CAST: Barbara Stanwyck, James Mason, Ava Gardner, Van Heflin, Cyd Charisse, Nancy Davis, William Conrad, Gale Sondergaard

THE FILE ON THELMA JORDON (Paramount, 1950)
PRODUCER: Hal B. Wallis
DIRECTOR: Robert Siodmak
SCREENPLAY: Ketti Frings
CAST: Barbara Stanwyck, Wendell Corey, Paul Kelly, Stanley Ridges, Joan Tetzel

NO MAN OF HER OWN (Paramount, 1950)
PRODUCER: Richard Maibaum
DIRECTOR: Mitchell Leisen
SCREENPLAY: Sally Benson, Catherine Turney
CAST: Barbara Stanwyck, John Lund, Phyllis Thaxter, Jane Cowl, Richard Denning, Milburn Stone, Lyle Bettger

THE FURIES (Paramount, 1950)
PRODUCER: Hal B. Wallis
DIRECTOR: Anthony Mann
SCREENPLAY: Charles Schnee
CAST: Barbara Stanwyck, Walter Huston, Wendell Corey, Judith Anderson, Beulah Bondi, Albert Dekker, Gilbert Roland

TO PLEASE A LADY (Metro-Goldwyn-Mayer, 1950)
PRODUCER: Clarence Brown
DIRECTOR: Clarence Brown
SCREENPLAY: Barré Lyndon, Marge Decker
CAST: Clark Gable, Barbara Stanwyck, Adolphe

Menjou, Will Geer, William C. McGaw, Roland Winters

THE MAN WITH A CLOAK (Metro-Goldwyn-Mayer, 1951)
PRODUCER: Stephen Ames
DIRECTOR: Fletcher Markle
SCREENPLAY: Frank Fenton
CAST: Joseph Cotten, Barbara Stanwyck, Louis Calhern, Leslie Caron, Jim Backus, Joe DeSantis

CLASH BY NIGHT (RKO, 1952)
EXECUTIVE
PRODUCERS: Jerry Wald, Norman Krasna
PRODUCER: Harriet Parsons
DIRECTOR: Fritz Lang
SCREENPLAY: Alfred Hays
CAST: Barbara Stanwyck, Robert Ryan, Paul Douglas, Marilyn Monroe, J. Carrol Naish, Keith Andes

JEOPARDY (Metro-Goldwyn-Mayer, 1953)
PRODUCER: Sol Baer Fielding
DIRECTOR: John Sturges
SCREENPLAY: Mel Dinelli
CAST: Barbara Stanwyck, Barry Sullivan, Ralph Meeker

TITANIC (Twentieth Century–Fox, 1953)
PRODUCER: Charles Brackett
DIRECTOR: Jean Negulesco
SCREENPLAY: Charles Brackett, Walter Reisch, Richard Breen
CAST: Clifton Webb, Barbara Stanwyck, Brian Aherne, Robert Wagner, Thelma Ritter, Audrey Dalton, Harper Carter, Richard Basehart

ALL I DESIRE   (Universal, 1953)
PRODUCER: Ross Hunter
DIRECTOR: Douglas Sirk
SCREENPLAY: James Gunn, Robert Blees
CAST: Barbara Stanwyck, Richard Carlson, Maureen O'Sullivan, Richard Long, Lyle Bettger, Marcia Henderson

THE MOONLIGHTER   (Warner Brothers, 1953)
PRODUCER: Joseph Bernhard
DIRECTOR: Roy Rowland
SCREENPLAY: Niven Busch
CAST: Barbara Stanwyck, Fred MacMurray, Ward Bond, Jack Elam

BLOWING WILD   (Warner Brothers, 1953)
PRODUCER: Milton Sperling
DIRECTOR: Hugo Fregonese
SCREENPLAY: Philip Yordan
CAST: Gary Cooper, Barbara Stanwyck, Ward Bond, Ruth Roman, Anthony Quinn, Ian MacDonald

WITNESS TO MURDER   (United Artists, 1954)
PRODUCER: Chester Erskine
DIRECTOR: Roy Rowland
SCREENPLAY: Chester Erskine
CAST: Barbara Stanwyck, George Sanders, Gary Merrill, Jesse White, Harry Shannon

EXECUTIVE SUITE   (Metro-Goldwyn-Mayer, 1954)
PRODUCER: John Houseman
DIRECTOR: Robert Wise
SCREENPLAY: Ernest Lehman
CAST: William Holden, June Allyson, Fredric March, Barbara Stanwyck, Walter Pidgeon, Shelley Winters, Paul Douglas, Louis Calhern, Nina Foch, Dean Jagger

CATTLE QUEEN OF MONTANA   (RKO, 1955)

PRODUCER: Benedict Bogeaus
DIRECTOR: Allan Dwan
SCREENPLAY: Howard Estabrook, Robert Blees
CAST: Barbara Stanwyck, Ronald Reagan, Jack Elam, Gene Evans, Lance Fuller, Anthony Caruso

THE VIOLENT MEN   (Columbia, 1955)

PRODUCER: Lewis J. Rachmil
DIRECTOR: Rudolph Maté
SCREENPLAY: Harry Kleiner
CAST: Glenn Ford, Barbara Stanwyck, Edward G. Robinson, Dianne Foster, Brian Keith, May Wynn

ESCAPE TO BURMA   (RKO, 1955)

PRODUCER: Benedict Bogeaus
DIRECTOR: Allan Dwan
SCREENPLAY: Talbot Jennings, Hobart Donavan
CAST: Barbara Stanwyck, David Farrar, Robert Ryan, Peter Coe, Reginald Denny

THERE'S ALWAYS TOMORROW (Universal, 1956)

PRODUCER: Ross Hunter
DIRECTOR: Douglas Sirk
SCREENPLAY: Bernard C. Schoenfeld
CAST: Barbara Stanwyck, Fred MacMurray, Joan Bennett, Pat Crowley, Jane Darwell

THE MAVERICK QUEEN   (Republic, 1956)

ASSOCIATE
PRODUCER: Joe Kane
DIRECTOR: Joe Kane
SCREENPLAY: Kenneth Gamet, DeVallon Scott
CAST: Barbara Stanwyck, Barry Sullivan, Scott Brady, Mary Murphy, Wallace Ford, Howard Petrie, Jim Davis

THESE WILDER YEARS   (Metro-Goldwyn-Mayer, 1956)

PRODUCER: Jules Schermer
DIRECTOR: Roy Rowland
SCREENPLAY: Frank Fenton
CAST: James Cagney, Barbara Stanwyck, Walter Pidgeon, Betty Lou Keim, Don Dubbins

CRIME OF PASSION   (United Artists, 1957)

EXECUTIVE
PRODUCER: Bob Goldstein
PRODUCER: Herman Cohen
DIRECTOR: Gerd Oswald
SCREENPLAY: Joe Eisinger
CAST: Barbara Stanwyck, Sterling Hayden, Raymond Burr, Fay Wray, Virginia Grey, Royal Dano

TROOPER HOOK   (United Artists, 1957)

PRODUCER: Sol Baer Fielding
DIRECTOR: Charles Marquis Warren
SCREENPLAY: Charles Marquis Warren, David Victor, and Herbert Little, Jr.
CAST: Joel McCrea, Barbara Stanwyck, Earl Holliman, Edward Andrews, John Dehner, Susan Kohner

FORTY GUNS   (Twentieth Century–Fox, 1957)

PRODUCER: Samuel Fuller
DIRECTOR: Samuel Fuller
SCREENPLAY: Samuel Fuller
CAST: Barbara Stanwyck, Barry Sullivan, Dean Jagger, John Ericson, Gene Barry, Robert Dix

WALK ON THE WILD SIDE   (Columbia, 1962)

PRODUCER: Charles K. Feldman
DIRECTOR: Edward Dmytryk

SCREENPLAY: John Fante, Edmund Morris
        CAST: Laurence Harvey, Capucine, Jane Fonda,
              Anne Baxter, Barbara Stanwyck, Donald
              Barry, Joanna Moore

ROUSTABOUT   (Paramount, 1964)
  PRODUCER: Hal B. Wallis
  DIRECTOR: John Rich
  SCREENPLAY: Anthony Lawrence, Allan Weiss
        CAST: Elvis Presley, Barbara Stanwyck, Joan
              Freeman, Leif Erickson, Sue Ann Lang-
              don, Pat Buttram

THE NIGHT WALKER   (Universal, 1965)
  PRODUCER: William Castle
  DIRECTOR: William Castle
  SCREENPLAY: Robert Bloch
        CAST: Robert Taylor, Barbara Stanwyck, Hay-
              den Rorke, Judith Meredith, Jess Barker,
              Lloyd Bochner

THE HOUSE THAT WOULDN'T DIE   (ABC Tele-
feature, 1970)
  PRODUCER: Aaron Spelling
  DIRECTOR: John Llewellyn Moxey
  TELEPLAY: Henry Farrell
        CAST: Barbara Stanwyck, Richard Egan, Michael
              Anderson, Jr., Katherine Winn, Doreen
              Lang, Mabel Albertson

A TASTE OF EVIL   (ABC Telefeature, 1971)
  PRODUCER: Aaron Spelling
  DIRECTOR: John Llewellyn Moxey
  TELEPLAY: Jimmy Sangster
        CAST: Barbara   Stanwyck,   Barbara   Parkins,
              Roddy   McDowall,   William   Windom,
              Arthur O'Connell, Bing Russell

THE LETTERS   (ABC Telefeature, 1973)

EXECUTIVE
PRODUCERS: Aaron Spelling, Leonard Goldberg
PRODUCER: Paul Junger Witt
DIRECTOR: Gene Nelson (Story 2)
TELEPLAY: Ellis Marcus, Hal Sitowitz
CAST: Story 1—John Forsythe, Jane Powell, Lesley Warren; Story 2—Barbara Stanwyck, Leslie Nielsen, Dina Merrill; Story 3—Ida Lupino, Ben Murphy, Pamela Franklin

THE THORN BIRDS   (ABC Miniseries, 1982)

EXECUTIVE
PRODUCERS: David L. Wolper, Edward Lewis
PRODUCER: Stan Margulies
DIRECTOR: Daryl Duke
TELEPLAY: Carmen Culver
CAST: Richard Chamberlain, Rachel Ward, Jean Simmons, Piper Laurie, Richard Kiley, Ken Howard, Christopher Plummer, Barbara Stanwyck